DEDICATION

*For my grandchildren, Rose, Sam, Layla, Adam,
Laurella and Coco, with the hope that they will always
indulge their curiosity and enjoy an open-minded
Spirit of Enquiry (for which Sam has, to my great
pride, just won his school prize!).*

Galileo
& The Art of
Ageing Mindfully
Wisdom from the Night Skies

Adam Ford

Leaping Hare Press

First published in the UK in 2015 by

Leaping Hare Press

210 High Street, Lewes
East Sussex BN7 2NS, UK
www.leapingharepress.co.uk

Text copyright © Adam Ford 2015
Design and layout copyright © Ivy Press Limited 2015

British Library Cataloguing-in-Publication Data
A catalogue record for this book is available from
the British Library

ISBN: 978-1-78240-243-5

This book was conceived, designed and produced by

Leaping Hare Press

Creative Director PETER BRIDGEWATER
Publisher SUSAN KELLY
Commissioning Editor MONICA PERDONI
Art Director WAYNE BLADES
Editorial Director TOM KITCH
Editor JENNI DAVIS
Designer GINNY ZEAL
Illustrator MELVYN EVANS

Printed in China
Colour origination by Ivy Press Reprographics

Distributed worldwide (except North America) by
Thames & Hudson Ltd., 181A High Holborn,
London WC1V 7QX, United Kingdom

1 3 5 7 9 10 8 6 4 2

Contents

Introduction 6

CHAPTER ONE
The Moving Earth 22

CHAPTER TWO
Who am I? 38

CHAPTER THREE
The Troubling Size of the Universe 50

CHAPTER FOUR
Mars, the Bringer of War 64

CHAPTER FIVE
Time Tunnels & Eternity 80

CHAPTER SIX
The Pull of Gravity 96

CHAPTER SEVEN
Are We Alone in the Universe 110

Endnotes 142
Bibliography 142
Acknowledgements 142
Index 143

INTRODUCTION

What are we to make of our brief lives in
this transitory world? They come and go so fast.
In childhood, time almost stands still — next Christmas
is an eternity away, a birthday party next week is an
age in coming. Then, as we grow older, time begins to
speed up — birthdays come round with accelerating
persistence; children we knew are suddenly middle-
aged. But growing older, I find, is full of unexpected
compensations. There is more time for living mindfully,
more time to think. There is time to pursue
interests squeezed out in a busy life —
in my case, the night sky.

PEACE FROM THE NIGHT SKY

◆

Studying the night sky absorbed me with a passion when I was young – and now, more than half a century later, I find that it still rests my spirit to look up and trace the pattern of the constellations, contemplate the distances of the stars and marvel at their immense age and the great voids that separate them.

IS IT ALREADY WEDNESDAY AGAIN? Growing older is a strange process. Time flies, a week passing in a flash: we who are older feel just the same as we did at seventeen – until we see some grey in the mirror or notice the skin on the back of our hands, a bit wrinkled and speckled ('Gosh! My hands are looking just like I remember my father's', I find myself thinking). I do a lot of walking, daily, and love it – and then I find myself toiling up a hill, legs heavy, pausing for breath, bewildered that an ordinary activity can be so exhausting. I have to laugh and learn how to take hills more slowly.

But I count myself as fortunate because, I have discovered that I have more time for conscious living, for practising mindfulness, for seeing things the way they are. The present moment becomes increasingly important, and there is something comforting about the physicality of my own body, even when it feels a bit challenged – I am breathing and alive. This all brings a change of focus on what is important in life, and helps me let go of things that are not worth worrying about.

One of my great pleasures is in having time to rediscover the night sky, something that has always fascinated me. The study of astronomy has a lot to tell us about who we are and how we came to be here on this small blue planet; we live in an extraordinary universe, unimaginably vast and ancient. Scientific enquiry and curiosity are part of the essence of being a human being and are in themselves spiritual activities. We now know, after centuries of research, that we are linked to all other evolving life on the planet, and have deep ties with the stars. It is this that I want to explore.

Brief Encounter

I think my awareness of these things began, if I can date it, with one of those fortunate and unplanned moments that litter our lives. I was nine years old and with my father visiting a friend of his, Tommy Hill, in Eskdale, a remote and beautiful valley in the north-west of England's Lake District, where I grew up. He owned a heavy pair of binoculars, captured (romantically, I remember thinking) from a German U-boat commander. We walked out into the garden at twilight and used the binoculars to gaze up at a half Moon through the branches of a copper beech tree. The leaves of the tree and the twigs became blurred as I adjusted the focus, and the Moon leapt into astonishing clarity, bright craters and black shadows. I was stunned, drawn into another world of sunlit landscapes, deep valleys and great mountain ranges.

The following morning I asked Miss Armstrong, our teacher in the very small village school in Boot, if I could tell the other children about the Moon. There were fourteen of us of all ages in the school and we did all our studies together, older children helping younger ones to read. A local shepherd, who sometimes brought his sheep to graze in the playground, a wild shoulder of land with outcropping rocks and bracken, called us respectfully 'the scholars'.

Taking up the chalk, I drew a large half Moon on the blackboard and then filled in masses of circles for the craters, each crater bigger than the Eskdale valley that was our world. I don't know what the other children made of it all, or what I said, but I tried to describe the mountainous and rugged lunar landscape as I had seen it. I had no words for the thrill the view had awakened in my heart.

I recently visited the spot where the Moon first revealed its face to me. The copper beech tree is still there, strangely looking no older than it did then, and peacefully linking childhood's astonishment with mindfulness in old age. The time has flown between then and now.

I drew a large half Moon on the blackboard and then filled in masses of circles for the craters.

A COMMUNITY OF CURIOSITY

◆

We are not alone in looking at the skies and asking ourselves questions – we come from a community of curiosity. We, in the twenty-first century, are inheritors of a wealth of information that comes from discoveries made by others.

F OR OVER FOUR HUNDRED YEARS astronomers have been exploring the heavens, making observations and gathering information, building scientific models of solar systems, stars and galaxies, speculating on how the universe came to be the way it is and, most importantly perhaps, investigating the story of how we came to be here. It is an epic tale, every bit as spiritual as it is scientific. Many scientists have had the experience that scientific research can itself be a form of religious contemplation. I have always found it difficult to understand why some people think that religion and science are at war with each other.

To remind myself that scientific research is a corporate activity, and that I only know what I know because of other people's curiosity and exploration, I want to tell this story in the company of the great astronomer Galileo Galilei.

About Galileo

Galileo was born in Pisa in 1564 (died in 1642) into a poor but cultured family of the lower Italian nobility. From his father he inherited radical views and a healthy contempt for authority, which he questioned at every available opportunity. He was appointed professor of mathematics at Pisa when he was twenty-five, three years later taking up a similar post in Padua in the Republic of Venice, where he remained for eighteen years. These years, he recollected in old age, were among the happiest in his life.

Galileo is often referred to as the Father of Modern Science. His experiments and investigations into optics and astronomy, into the motion of falling objects and the movement of the tides, into the swing of pendulums and the flight of cannon balls, were all part of a bright new way of looking at the world, observing things as they *are* – rather than how we have been *told* they are. Experiment replaced prejudice; clear mindful wakefulness replaced blind repetition. We began to wake up to and understand our place in the universe.

In most people's minds, Galileo's name is associated with his famous trial by the Roman Catholic Inquisition. Sadly, he is remembered as much for this clash with authority as he is for his world-changing discoveries; some claims about the way he was treated by the Church have become exaggerated. He is often dragged into the argument for atheism, as 'proof' that religion has always opposed the advance of scientific knowledge. The reality was much more complex. He was a difficult man, quick-thinking and prone to mocking anyone who disagreed with him, creating enemies and admirers at every turn; and he certainly suffered a long argument with some people in authority in the Roman Catholic Church. We will see why this was so later as we contemplate some of the implications of what he discovered with his telescope. Throughout all his troubles, however, Galileo remained a good Catholic to the end of his life and received great support from his religiously devout and adoring daughter Sister Maria Celeste, a nun, with whom he had a lifelong correspondence.

Galileo was a man after my own heart, with priorities that I greatly admire. He refused, for example, to wear the regulation academic dress in Pisa at all times (cumbersome when climbing the famous leaning tower to conduct experiments with falling objects!), deeming the official doctoral dress a pretentious nuisance. He delighted in the singing of birds, observing that they could transform the air they breathed into 'a variety of sweet songs'. He loved wine, describing it as 'light held together by moisture'. And believing that his discoveries should be made available to the common man, he wrote his books in the vulgar tongue rather than in Latin, the language of the Church.

Galileo's Telescope

Contrary to the belief of some writers in the past, Galileo did not invent the telescope: the accolade for that must go to Hans Lippershey, a spectacle-maker in the Netherlands. In 1608, while experimenting with the property that glass has for bending (refracting) light rays, Lippershey discovered that a convex lens viewed through a concave lens produced a magnified image of distant objects. Galileo's strength and genius was in seeing the potential of this great discovery. He seized the day, constructed his own telescope and pointed it at the stars. But that was only after he had tried to sell the invention to powerful ship owners in Venice, for whom it would offer a great trading advantage to be able to identify ships on the horizon, before others got wind of their arrival.

It was in 1609 that Galileo first turned his small handmade instrument on the heavens, and it was a mindfulness moment for mankind. He was doing something no one had done before, and after gazing out at the universe for several nights he knew that what he saw would change history and alter the way we think about ourselves for ever. He was right. This was a great period in history – in England, Shakespeare was at the height of his career and the Pilgrim Fathers were soon to depart to their New World.

The story of Galileo and his telescope – his discovery of the moons of Jupiter, and the mountain ranges on our own Moon, of spots on the Sun, and stars in the Milky Way, of the moon-like phases of Venus – I take as a sort of parable. The process of facing reality, coming to terms with our place in the universe, that began at the macro level for mankind four hundred years ago is reflected at the micro level in our own individual lives. How do we belong in this ancient cosmos?

I write this at a time in life by which age Galileo, sadly, had gone blind, and could no longer see those skies that had brought him such fame. The notorious trial by the Inquisition, for claiming among other things that the Earth moved, lay in the past; he lived under house arrest and his devoted daughter Sister Maria Celeste had died four years earlier from dysentery. 'This universe,' he wrote in a letter to a friend in 1638, 'which I with astonishing observations and clear demonstrations had enlarged a hundred, nay, a thousandfold beyond the limits commonly seen by wise men of all centuries past, is now for me so diminished and reduced, it has shrunk to the meagre confines of my body.'[1]

Growing Old With the Stars

We all face, with Galileo, the inevitable limitations of growing older. I find calm in contemplating the skies at night – the meditation puts things into perspective, encouraging an inner stillness. I can then reflect, with greater strength and confidence, on the brevity of life – particularly when viewed against the cosmic backdrop revealed by Galileo's telescope. The universe is almost unimaginably ancient; our lives, even at the biblical 'three score years and ten' (which I have already passed), are mere flickers of consciousness in comparison.

Astronomy is a good place to start when thinking about these things. You do not need, yourself, to peer through the great telescopes high above the clouds in Hawaii, Chile or

Tenerife, to think about the stars or the nature of eternity. The truths of astronomy can be absorbed even without a telescope; we only have to step outside at night, giving ourselves time to stand and stare while breathing the delicious night air.

No star maps come with this book and it can easily be read without them. All you need is imagination and some time to contemplate ideas. I will, however, be referring to particular stars, planets and constellations and will provide enough description to help you find them during the year. A simple guide to the stars, available from most good bookshops or through the internet, will help, of course. Many newspapers provide useful monthly star maps.

THE NEXT GENERATION

◆

As a grandfather, I would love to pass something on to my grandchildren — and I don't just mean money. I respect the wisdom of previous generations and would like to contribute to this conversation with my descendents — it takes more than one lifetime to understand this world, to glimpse its whispered wisdom.

As I write, I also want to reflect on what messages I would like to pass on to my grandchildren (let's not call it advice). We each of us live on a learning curve marked by experiences that can be worth sharing. My father was a country parson and I grew up with a sister and three brothers, living mostly in Cumbria in the north of England. Always interested in astronomy, I nevertheless switched to theology and philosophy at university and progressed to being an Anglican vicar of a mill town in Yorkshire. From there I became chaplain in a London school where, alongside religious studies, I taught astronomy. I have now retired and live with my wife, Ros, in a beautiful village in the South Downs, where I walk daily. Six marvellous grandchildren are now the pride of my life (along with my four children and their partners).

It can be difficult being a human being. Each of us begins from scratch, blinking, trying to make sense of the world, and then as our minds begin to pick up on language, we collect ideas about how to behave, how to relate to those other worlds around us that we call 'people', testing our parents to see what we can get away with, how far we can go with selfish behaviour; collapsing into tantrums when things don't work out quite as we would like. This process does not end in childhood and often remains unexplained.

Am I wiser being older? I can't claim that for myself, but I do think that I see the way things are more clearly. I have always tended to shy away from giving advice to others, and yet it does seem worthwhile to pass on some thoughts to my grandchildren – which they can take or leave, as they wish. Some of these thoughts are scattered throughout the book, with the hope that they may be of help. One of the few bits of advice my own mother gave me was: 'Don't worry about

Notes to Grandchildren

• A scientific explanation of anything in this world, or of the world itself, should not deny a spiritual view of things. Otherwise it is impoverished and untrue.

• Many truths lie beyond words; as in music, beauty and the meaning of our lives.

• Beware any world view that claims to be the only true one, whether it originates from a fundamentalist scientist or a religious extremist.

• Follow and indulge your interests throughout your life — when you retire from full-time work they will be invaluable and may lead to projects such as travel, research, and the acquiring of new skills (to paint, draw, make music...)

what other people think of you — just be yourself.' I have valued the thought. Less valuable was my father's advice, given when attempting to deliver a 'sex talk' in my teens: 'Beware of enthusiastic amateurs!' I was never quite sure what he was talking about — but hindsight suggests it had to do with his fear that a son of his might get a girl pregnant!

THE ORIGINS OF MINDFULNESS

◆

The practice of mindfulness has two roots, one historic and the other internal. It would be negligent of us not to recollect, now and then, that the practice is not a modern invention or fashion but stems from an ancient spiritual tradition.

MINDFULNESS HAS BECOME POPULAR recently and much used by psychiatrists, quite rightly, as a therapeutic technique in helping people with mental or emotional problems; short courses are offered all over the country, for those who want to find ways to relieve some of the stresses of everyday life, to cope with anxiety or the troubling demands of work. Even groups of MPs in the houses of Westminster have been meeting for mindfulness training.

Its origins, however, lie two and a half thousand years ago in Buddhism – but although mindfulness has its origins in religion (where it is known as *Samma Sati,* or right awareness, and is the seventh step in the Buddhist Noble Eightfold Path leading to calm, insight, enlightenment, and ultimately to Nirvana), it is not in itself a religious activity. Anyone can benefit from its practice, whether atheist, Christian, Jew, Muslim or adherent to any other religion or philosophy. It is a physical/spiritual exercise open to all.

The original Buddha's teaching was a practical way to cope with the problems of being a human, often dominated by greed anger or ignorance. 'Wake up to your condition and follow a path that will lead to a better way of being.'

Taking Responsibility

The Buddha warned us not to be led blindly by others. It is recorded that he was once visiting some people in the north Indian kingdom of Kosala, when they asked him for his advice. Apparently they were surrounded by many different sects, teachers and holy men, who all seemed not only to disagree with one another, but spent a lot of time despising and condemning the doctrines of others. How could they distinguish truth from falsehood, they asked?

His advice was that they should take responsibility for themselves. Test the teaching, taste it. Don't accept a doctrine simply because someone with authority teaches it, or because it is to be found in a religious text – not even if the Buddha teaches it. 'But... when you know for yourselves that certain things are unwholesome and wrong, and bad, then give them up... and when you know for yourselves that certain things are wholesome and good, then accept them and follow them.'[2]

So it is with the practice of mindfulness. The awakening of awareness can be found through focusing on the body and its breathing in the present moment, whether walking, standing, sitting or lying down. It involves paying attention *now* to physical feelings, to sensations, emotions and thoughts.

Mindfulness for All Ages

The second root of mindfulness lies already within ourselves: it is the capacity to awake for a moment with a sense of wonder, noticing the present moment with gratitude, while adopting a calm acceptance of the way things are. This is something we experienced naturally in childhood but have often forgotten. It strikes me sometimes that this is what Jesus may have meant when he taught that 'unless you accept the kingdom of heaven as a little child you can never enter it'.

I recently stood by a window and watched my two-year-old grandson, Adam, playing out in the garden. Most of the time he was running about, chasing his sister, climbing over his grandfather, demanding attention from his mother, and so forth, in continuous noisy activity. Now for a moment he was on his own, just sitting on the lawn, watching birds fly overhead and smiling to himself. His podgy hand clutched a japonica fruit he had found on the lawn. He tested it, licked and tried to bite it – it was so like an apple – but to no avail. Then a burst of wind stirred the trees in the garden and he looked up. The branches of a tall eucalyptus in the neighbour's garden swayed, waving in the heavy gust, bending towards him. Adam put down the piece of hard fruit, hesitated a moment and then waved back at the tree.

That, I am sure, was a mindfulness moment, wakeful and absorbed in the present, though Adam had no words to describe or acknowledge it.

CHAPTER ONE

THE MOVING EARTH

*There is so much movement in the world today
that we scarcely give it a second thought. Many of us
commute to work daily by bus, train, or bicycle; we 'pop
down to the shops' for the slightest needs; TV brings
images into our homes of football teams sprinting up
and down a pitch after a ball, or athletes belting
round a track. We drive for miles to see friends at
weekends or fly away to foreign parts on holiday;
a select few have even flown to the Moon. But it
was ideas about movement that got Galileo into
so much trouble with the Inquisition.*

GROWING OLD MINDFULLY

◆

Feeling upset about getting old and not being able to move as fast as we might like to is futile — one might as well rage against gravity or against the north-east wind. Mindfulness practice faces reality graciously. It is, after all, a privilege in this dangerous world to have reached old age at all.

W E ARE ALL ON A TRAJECTORY THROUGH LIFE, learning to accept its various episodes and critical turning points. One of the most challenging periods for many people is the transition from a full-time working life to retirement. The clue, I think, is not to think of this new stage in one's career as retirement at all, but to seize it by the horns and welcome the opportunities it offers. My own solution was to plan a 'gap' year, just like my students did when leaving school. I made a short list of goals I wanted to accomplish: to see an albatross; to sit at the foot of a monolithic head on Easter Island; to stare across the Nullarbor Plain in South Australia; and to see the southern stars, constellations never visible from northern Europe.

My travels lived up to all that I had hoped for, and the southern stars were as pleasing as I had expected. The Southern Cross was as prominent as it appears on the Australian flag. Other travellers had sought out this constellation long before me, as a guide when sailing southern seas, some being led astray by a similar group of stars dubbed the 'False Cross'. I also found the very beautiful Canopus, the second brightest star in the whole sky: it lies well to the south of Orion and is never visible from British latitudes. Canopus shines in the constellation of Carina, the Keel, one of three groups of stars that used to bear the name of Argo, the Ship, named after the fifty-oared vessel that carried Jason and the Argonauts on their legendary voyage to find the Golden Fleece. Canopus was always thought to be the pilot of the star ship, though it is also claimed that it was he who piloted the fleet of Menelaus to Egypt after the destruction of Troy; he died there and a town was named after him. It satisfied me greatly to discover later, when talking with an astronaut, that Canopus had been a guide star for the Apollo missions to the Moon.

Our Daily Movement Through the Heavens

It may be because of this inevitable slowing down that I find myself contemplating more often the ceaseless movement of the heavens. In the universe, everything is in motion all the time – at speeds that blow the mind. It was thinking about aspects of this movement that disturbed many people in Galileo's day; it rocked their world. They shared the conviction of the author of Psalm 104, that the Lord had '…laid the foundation of the Earth: that it never should move at any time'. But something Galileo had seen through his small hand-held telescope forced them to face up to reality.

MINDFULNESS EXERCISE

FEELING THE EARTH TURN

Take time off and walk outside on a clear night; let the eyes adjust to the dark. This may take five minutes or so. If you live in a city where it is never entirely dark, don't worry – it will not affect the observations you are about to make. Do a breathing exercise, gently emptying the lungs then slowly breathing in; relax the belly and let the breath go deep. Don't force it, let it all come naturally and be aware of this lovely life-giving process. The breath flows in and the breath flows out.

Without rushing, extend this awareness throughout the body, feeling the night air on the skin, hearing a dog bark in the distance, the sound of a car moving away. Open the shoulders, stand a bit straighter, feet planted firmly on the ground, and feel the comforting drag of gravity as the planet pulls us towards its centre.

Select a star – or the Moon – low near the horizon, preferably to the east or the west (the east being where the Sun rises, remember, and sets in the west!). It could be any star, though in winter in the northern hemisphere you might choose Sirius, known as the Dog Star; it is the brightest star in the whole sky and twinkles brilliantly, flashing ruby and emerald as the light coruscates through our turbulent atmosphere.

Now watch. Let the star, or Moon, become part of your awareness of the present moment as you stand centred in your breathing body. Notice the star's position. Try to line it up with a chimney pot or branch of a tree. Stand and stare. Continue to be aware of your breathing and of the pull of gravity, with your feet firmly planted on the ground.

After only a few minutes, if you have managed to keep still, you will notice something: the star has moved as it slowly swings up and away from the horizon as it rises, or down to the horizon as it sets. It is slow, like watching the hour hand of a clock, which seems to be stationary but quietly moves relentlessly on. There has been movement; but whose movement?

All the stars and planets, and the Moon, sail across the sky at night in the same direction as the Sun tracks during the day. And of course we all know why. The Earth is turning. But when we are watching that star disappearing behind a chimney pot or emerging from behind the branch of a tree silhouetted against the sky, we are likely to think 'Oh! It has moved' and give no thought to the fact that actually it was the chimney pot or the branch that has moved. They are attached through the house or the tree to the landscape around us, or to the city, and fixed to the surface of the planet. We stand breathing on a turning Earth.

If you live in the latitude of London, then the world is quietly carrying you around on its daily carousel at about 800 kilometres (500 miles) per hour; if you live in the tropics then it is nearer 1,600 kilometres (1,000 miles) per hour. It will take time, in this exercise, to begin to feel that it is *we* who are moving, as stars, planets and Moon *seem* to rise and set.

I first experienced this feeling of the turning world when standing on a hill in my teens in Cumbria. I watched the winter constellation of Orion setting beyond the Solway Plain over the Irish Sea. Then the truth began to seep into my bones; Cumbria was quietly, with a relentless swing, tilting away from the west, lifting the horizon against the sky, slowly hiding Orion, the giant, from the feet upwards.

We have all known, we 'modern' people, probably since we were in our first school, that the world is a globe that is suspended in space and turns on its axis once in twenty-four hours. This was a thought that worried the ancients before the birth of modern science. The great astronomer Ptolemy, in the second century BC, believed we would all be buffeted by a great wind if the Earth turned, the clouds would race across the sky and all the birds would be blown away in a permanent hurricane. It was common sense. He knew from measurements made by Greek astronomers that the world was very big (almost 13,000 kilometres – or just under 8,000 miles – in diameter); the thought of such a massive body actually *turning* seemed to make no sense at all, particularly as it didn't *feel* as if it was turning. One and a half millennia later, Nicolaus Copernicus (of whom we will hear more later) pointed out that the air travelled with the rotating globe, just as easily and naturally as his coat stayed wrapped around him as he walked down the street. The air shares our turning momentum and so the birds and clouds do not get left behind.

With the accumulated wisdom of science behind us, we now know with our heads that the world spins on its axis once a day, carrying the clouds, the birds and the air with it. But do we actually believe it and feel it in our bones? On pages 26–27, there is a mindfulness exercise we can practise to get things moving, as it were, even if we have taken to resting more than we used to when we were younger.

AN OLD PRINT FROM MY CHILDHOOD'S BEDROOM WALL

◆

I treasure a picture that has been with me from as far back as I can remember. My mother bought it in a junk shop and hung it on my bedroom wall, perhaps seventy years ago. Today, it hangs with comforting familiarity in my study, where I write.

T HE LARGE FRAME IS OLD, MOULDED AND GILDED, the gilt flaking off in places to reveal white plaster. It hangs somewhat precariously from screws in the back and a stretch of badly knotted fishing line. The picture, in greys, soft blues and greens, is a print taken from an eighteenth- or perhaps even seventeenth-century Dutch book and looks, from a distance, rather like a dartboard. There are inscriptions in Latin.

It is a diagram of the (then) new model of the solar system with the Sun at the centre orbited by the planets, including our own terra firma, as proposed by Nicolaus Copernicus at about the same time as Christopher Columbus, confident that the world was round, was sailing the ocean blue and discovering the New World. Copernicus was not a brave man, and has

Christopher Columbus, confident that the world was round, was sailing the ocean blue and discovering the New World.

been described as 'the timid canon'. He was appointed to a canonry in the cathedral of Frauenburg, Poland, but kept well out of the public eye, living in a tower on a reasonable clerical stipend and focusing on the mathematics of planetary motion. Our timid canon was deeply anxious that he would be 'hissed off the stage' for his preposterous proposal that the Earth moved, not just by turning on its axis, but also in orbiting the Sun. Mathematically it made absolute sense, but he knew it would offend deeply ingrained habits of thinking.

The World in My Picture

The centre of my picture is dominated by the Sun with a hint of a smile on its calm face; the Sun's rays radiate out almost to the limits of the print, producing the dartboard effect. Concentric circles, like ripples from a splash, spread outwards, marking the orbits of the known planets from Mercury to Saturn. Earth has pride of place in the twelve o'clock position – a sphere with a tiny coloured map of the world, Africa and Asia named. A ring of blue surrounds it, providing the only splash of colour among the subdued tones of the print. Then the Moon has its own small orbit around the Earth. The other planets are represented by small multi-rayed stars.

Around this solar system there is a belt of mottled green cloud, containing the twelve signs of the zodiac, each sign illustrated – Scorpio, for example, with a vicious curving tail and sting at the top; Gemini the Twins standing shoulder to shoulder at the bottom; Taurus the Bull charging out of the clouds, snorting. Two figures sit bottom right and left of the picture, philosophers draped in the folds of heavy medieval clothes, their hands resting on globes: one holds a compass. Is this Copernicus himself? And is the other Galileo?

My eye has always been drawn to the formal depiction of Jupiter, the largest of the planets in the solar system. IVPITER is inscribed in Latin around part of the orbit, its lettering like something on an old gravestone. The planet itself is represented by a star flanked by four other stars; together they look like the dots on a dice for the number five. It was this image that shook the world so seismically in the seventeenth century – for this is what Galileo saw through his small hand-held telescope.

Galileo Sees the Moons of Jupiter…

Copernicus had demonstrated mathematically that the planets orbit the Sun and not the Earth: he set the Earth free to move in space. Our world was no longer at the centre of the cosmos. In 1609, Galileo turned his newly invented telescope (a copy of the prototype built by Hans Lippershey) on Jupiter and saw to his great surprise that it moved against the background of stars in company with what at first looked like four small stars. Observations made over a few days revealed that they were moons in orbit around the great planet. Here, with this simple fact, was a clear demonstration that not everything orbits our world. It was earth-shattering news. Many refused to believe the evidence, arguing that there was probably a fault with Galileo's telescope. Galileo is quoted, perhaps apocryphally, as saying that he hoped they would pass Jupiter on their way to heaven when they died, and see the four orbiting moons for themselves.

...And So Do I

I first saw the moons of Jupiter when I was twelve years old and had begun to take a serious interest in astronomy. I borrowed books from the local library and began to learn the names of the constellations. It was a monthly chart in a newspaper that alerted me to the current position of Jupiter. It did not rise at that time of the year until just after midnight and was to be found in the constellation of Gemini. My alarm clock woke me at four o'clock in the morning and I crept out of the house, hoping not to wake my parents or siblings.

I can replay this experience in all its detail well over half a century later. Closing the back door quietly, I walked around a wing of the house to the vegetable garden. The sky was clear, a vault of stars arcing up from the avenue of elm trees that ran along a neighbouring drive. And there was Jupiter. I hadn't expected it to be so bright – a shining pearl, untwinkling, among the fainter stars of Gemini. It was so beautiful that I just stared at it for a long time before raising my binoculars and focusing. Three moons, spread out in a straight line, flanked the planet, two to the right and one far to the left; a mini solar system. The fourth, I supposed, must be behind the body of Jupiter. Known as the Galilean moons, they have been given lovely names, Io, Callisto, Ganymede and Europa – all from Greek mythology.

Rising in the small hours several times during the next few days, I followed the moons with my binoculars as they swung round their parent body. I can imagine the thrill for Galileo when he first observed what was happening – and the tremendous implications for mankind's understanding of its place in the world. Here was the first piece of evidence – four small worlds orbiting another world – that we were not at the centre of the universe. Perhaps it was true that our world also moved through space with its own moon – people weren't sure what to think about it. In 1600, Galileo's contemporary Giordano Bruno, a Dominican friar, was burnt to death at the stake in Rome by the Inquisition for teaching the heresy that the Earth moved and orbited the Sun. This inevitably made Galileo cautious. But does it really matter, some people began to ask, that we are not at the centre of the cosmos?

I can imagine the thrill for Galileo when he first observed what was happening.

Disappointment for Galileo

Sadly for Galileo, the knock-down evidence needed to dem-
onstrate the annual movement of the Earth around the Sun
did not come in his lifetime. In his book *Dialogue on the Two
Great World Systems*, he had proposed an experiment to reveal
this movement – as the Earth orbits the Sun, the closest stars
should appear to nod from side to side as they are displaced
against the background of more distant stars, in a phenomenon called 'parallax'. Such delicate measurements were not
possible in Galileo's time, the distances being so great and the
parallax so small. It was not until two hundred years later that
astronomical instruments were able to make such fine observations, vindicating his theory.

BACK TO THE PRESENT

◆

*It is easy for us as we grow older to become a bit fixated on the ways
by which we measure the flow of time, in weeks and months and
years: the measurements seem artificial when we consider the slow
movements of some planets.*

JUPITER, AS I WRITE, is back in the constellation of Gemini
where it was when I first saw it. It is high in the evening
twilight now, straight above my house. It has orbited the Sun
five times since I was twelve years old, tracking slowly
through the twelve signs of the zodiac, taking roughly twelve

Earth years to complete each circuit. That makes me about six years old – in Jupiter years. The passing of time and our method of marking it becomes a bit meaningless at the thought, just a way of pointing at the present.

I showed Jupiter to my granddaughter, Layla, before she went home with her mother one evening. 'Look,' I said, calling her attention to the sky above the house, 'I first saw that bright planet when I was a boy of twelve, five years ago.' She thought for a moment with a slightly worried expression; she had become proud of her new knowledge of numbers. 'Grandpa – you weren't a boy of twelve just five years ago! You were much older than that!' Having doubted my sanity, she was relieved when I explained. I now wonder if I will still be around next time the planet is in Gemini. I will be seven years old by then!

Looking to the Past & Future

We all of us live in the present moment, turning our minds continually to the past and the future, to search for memories from one while anticipating the unknown in the other – as I have just been doing, recollecting my life against the back-drop of Jupiter's slow progress around the heavens. Many older people who write about the slowing trajectory of their lives observe that they spend less time looking forward to the future and much more looking back to the past. This, I find, is only partially true. We certainly do have more time to dwell on memories, to indulge and enjoy them; these essential threads of remembered events contribute to our sense of self.

The future has contracted as I have grown older and is no longer that endless dream of youth. Its unknown end has become a real and close horizon – which does not trouble me at all. But though I have less years ahead of me than those that lie behind me, I still find myself looking forward with pleasure and happy anticipation, mostly to small things – fish and chips with a glass of wine by the sea with Ros, my wife; a trip up to London to visit an art exhibition with Imogen, my daughter; or a planned picnic somewhere up on the South Downs. I sometimes do wonder (hopefully) whether I shall see Jupiter pass through Gemini for a seventh time; visit Australia again to see the Spotted Pardelot, one of my favourite small birds, in the eucalyptus forests of the Blue Mountains; and be around to see, and maybe even conduct, the weddings of my various grandchildren. The lack of certainty about these things though is not, I am relieved to be able to say, a cause of any anxiety. I am sure this has to be one of the fruits of learning to enjoy the present moment: *this* is where I am, breathing comfortably, conscious that I am alive, finding fulfilment and peace in the here and now.

> *The future has contracted as I have grown older and is no longer that endless dream of youth.*

A Further Thought About Movement

In an exercise described earlier, we tried to get the *feel* of something we have known rationally to be true for years — that we live on a turning planet. We are moving all the time, far faster than any high-speed train. But that was nothing. The Copernican Revolution, which gave us a new way of thinking about our place in the universe and which Galileo began to confirm with his telescope, taught us that the Earth orbits the Sun in a year. Next time you are aware of the Sun in the sky, just think for a moment: wherever it is you plan to be in six months' time, whether at home gardening, travelling in a gap year or maybe fulfilling a long-standing wish to walk in a desert, one thing is for sure — you will be on the far side of the Sun, roughly 300 million kilometres (186 million miles) away from where you are now. To make that journey, spaceship Earth has to travel unrelentingly at 30 kilometres (18 miles) a second. (If you look towards the Sun from the northern hemisphere, then we are travelling around it to the right.)

CHAPTER TWO

WHO AM I?

Who are we? We who drive buses or teach
children in schools; we who mine the Earth and
plough the fields, paint pictures and make music; we
who work in air-conditioned offices or sleep rough on
the streets. We who grow old — who are we? And what
are we doing here on this small, rocky planet? There
are connections, so often ignored, that link us to
everything else in the universe, to all other living
things, to the periodic table of elements, to the Sun,
Moon and stars; these links and relationships
are strong and ancient.

RIGHT VIEWS

'Who am I?' has to be one of the most difficult questions to answer in the practice of mindfulness – not necessarily because we don't know, for we have, after all, lived in our own company ever since we first became conscious. It is a question that can become particularly tantalizing as we grow older.

WE KNOW WHO WE ARE: but how do we explore this instinctive knowledge with words? I am the conscious centre of my own world; but who *is* that? The name, Adam, I was given at birth over seventy years ago does not help – it sticks like a label on the outside of the mystery that is my own secret self.

Some people will want to answer the question in terms of the spiritual tradition that has guided their thinking throughout life – I am an immortal soul seeking freedom from ignorance, stuck in the round of rebirth, being reincarnated again and again; or, I am a child of God, redeemed and saved by his son Jesus Christ. These traditions all offer a narrative to explain who we are and to give us direction in our lives; in Buddhism, this would be called having Right Views and form one of the elements in the Noble Eightfold Path along with *Samma Sati*, Right Mindfulness. For the Buddha, Right Views involved acknowledging that dis-ease and pain run right through life; that the suffering is generated by greed, anger and ignorance; and that the proper way forward is to follow the Eightfold Path to calm, enlightenment and ultimately to Nirvana. There is no mention in Buddhism of a divine creator.

We will all, inevitably, bring our own 'right views' system to our practice of mindfulness, the Christian no less than the atheist, the Jew, Muslim, Hindu or Buddhist.

We Are Part of a Cosmic Process

These arresting words were written by the son of a Hereford shoemaker in the seventeenth century: Thomas Traherne, an Anglican priest and metaphysical poet who saw little of his work published in his own lifetime. He led a simple and devout life, owning little more, it is said, than some books and his old hat. His brand of mysticism, finding glory in creation, is reminiscent of Gerard Manley Hopkins, William Blake and Walt Whitman. His sense of 'oneness' with all things is a recognizable mark of mysticism the world over, whatever its religious source.

◆

You never enjoy the world aright, until the sea itself floweth through your veins, till you are clothed with the heavens and crowned with the stars, and perceive yourself to be the sole heir of the whole world...

FROM 'DIVINE RAPTURES'
THOMAS TRAHERNE (c.1637–1674)

◆

MINDFULNESS EXERCISE

MEDITATION ON A STAR

We need to think slowly about the fact that we are all made from star material, taking time to absorb its meaning. I suggest we choose a star in one of our night-time meditations, and contemplate its distant twinkling light. It doesn't matter which star — you may already have a favourite, perhaps Polaris above the North Pole, or Vega in the constellation of Lyra, high overhead in the northern hemisphere in August. But you don't even have to know the name of your star, or which constellation it belongs to. An anonymous star will do just as well.

I am going to choose Betelgeuse, the bright red star in the top left (as we look at him) shoulder of Orion on a winter's night. Orion, in one of the finest patches of the night sky to be seen, straddles the celestial equator and is just as well viewed from Australia, but upside down and in summer. Betelgeuse is a 'red-giant' type of star almost five hundred light years away (something we will explore later); it is enormous and over three hundred times the diameter of our own local star, the Sun.

First, while allowing the eyes to adjust to the dark, find a comfortable standing poise (or sitting, if you prefer) and quietly do the breathing exercise, focusing on the cool night air as it flows into and out of the lungs. Feel the pull of gravity through your feet, rooting you to the spot. Note, but dismiss, passing thoughts or worries in favour of being aware in the present moment, here… and now. Allow yourself the luxury of permitting time to hang still for a little while — a calming and awakening interlude in your evening. Say to yourself: 'This is it — I am here.'

Now let your focus settle on your chosen star. It is made mostly from hydrogen and helium, the simplest of the elements in the periodic table, but it will also contain an extra smattering of heavier elements, carbon, oxygen, iron and so forth – and also traces of other even more massive atoms, such as gold. The oldest stars in the universe did not contain these extra elements: it took hundreds of millions of years, in the extreme pressures and temperatures at a star's core, to forge the heavier atoms, building them by nuclear fusion from the simpler 'atomic building bricks' in the star's deep atmosphere: two hydrogen atoms to make a helium atom, three helium atoms to make a carbon atom and so on up the scale of massiveness in the periodic table.

We would not be here without the carbon for our bodies, forged at the heart of a stellar furnace; without the haemoglobin for our blood; or without the oxygen in the cool night air that we are now breathing in and out of our lungs.

But all this material, the carbon, oxygen, iron, and so forth, essential for our lives, would have been useless if it had all remained locked up in the stellar nuclear furnaces; it had to be liberated from the stars some-how, in order to be here in the ground of our planet, ready for life to evolve and, over time, for us to emerge from the process. For that to happen, ancient stars had to explode as Novae or Supernovae, blazing for several weeks brighter, sometimes, than a billion suns, distributing their material throughout interstellar space in tenuous clouds of dust and gas.

What the mystics grasped intuitively, modern science shows to be true – we are not isolated units in an unfriendly universe, but are part of an extraordinary web of relationships and connections that link us individually to everything else, in a creative activity that has been taking place from deep geological time to the present day.

A cosmic process flows through us; any feelings of isolation are a product of human delusion. Traherne could write 'until the sea itself floweth through your veins, till you are clothed with the heavens and crowned with the stars' from his instinctive awareness of the links that bind us to everything else in nature – even to the sun and stars. What he could not know, living in the seventeenth century, is that the essential iron in the haemoglobin of our blood was forged in the nuclear furnaces deep in the hearts of ancient suns, stars that lit the cosmic clouds long before our own star, the Sun, was born. Iron from the stars flows through our veins.

The Long Life of Star Dust

Heavier elements of a star's interior can also escape by being churned upwards towards the surface by forces deep within a stellar giant such as Betelgeuse (the star I chose for my mindfulness exercise on pages 42–43), finally to be carried into space by hot winds that spread them out to drift for aeons through the void, until the forces of gravity pull them together to make other suns and planets. We now realize that the atoms that make up our bodies have a long and glorious history; for a brief moment in their cosmic journey they are brought together to make you and me. We are temporary structures – but as it has been noted, we are made from star dust.

After many millions of years, drifting through the dark reaches of space, this star dust became embroiled in the creation of the solar system some four and a half billion years ago as gravity pulled it together to form the Sun and planets. Only then could it begin an extraordinary and creative history on Earth. Primo Levi, in his lovely book *The Periodic Table*,[3] writes a fictitious but entirely plausible biography of a single life-giving carbon atom. Carbon atoms have the unique ability to form molecular chains with other atoms and are essential for the growth of all living things, including our bodies.

The Carbon Atom's Journey

Levi's carbon atom, in his micro-history, is entrapped for millions of years in a limestone cliff; from there it is released by a hammer and taken to a lime kiln where it escapes into the air, joining with two oxygen atoms to become carbon dioxide. It travels around the world many times in the atmosphere, until it finds its way into the soil in Italy and becomes part of a vine, and so through a grape into a glass of wine. Someone gives a toast and the atom enters a human body. It is by such a means, through the food we eat and the drink we consume, that carbon becomes part of us.

It is entirely possible, and indeed very likely, that some of the carbon atoms in the skin on the back of your hand spent time in the bodies of dinosaurs, or in wayside flowers – a dog rose, perhaps, or a shy violet. And some of the carbon atoms in your brain, those that make it possible to read this text, spent a period of their history in the first single-celled creatures that populated the oceans three billion years ago.

RIGHT VIEWS: SCIENTIFIC & SPIRITUAL

Life on earth is in essence a recycling process, and always has been. Whatever our own spiritual or philosophical tradition, it is helpful to practise mindfulness with this knowledge. If we are to understand our lives better, that understanding should include, at the very least, the basic facts of our physical existence.

WE ARE MADE FROM ANCIENT RECYCLED MATERIAL that came from the stars. Our bodies grow old but not the particles from which they are made. A new meaning is added to the traditional words of the funeral 'ashes to ashes; dust to dust'. Star dust to star dust.

That star you chose to contemplate – you have a lot in common with it. Focus again mindfully on your breath, inhaled and exhaled in a gentle rhythm; flowing into you, it brings oxygen you need to invigorate your blood, oxygen originally from the stars; exhaled, it contains a trace of carbon dioxide, which your lungs cannot use, but is necessary for the leaves in the garden, and the trees. They will make use of it for its carbon to build new living cells, through the chemical miracle of photosynthesis – and in so doing, will release more of the oxygen we breathe.

For me, meditating within the Christian tradition, I find stirring resonances with the doctrine of the incarnation – that Jesus, as our prototype of a human being, was the Divine 'made flesh'. There is something quite remarkable about the flesh of each of us – and even more, perhaps, in what emerges from it, whether we call it soul or spirit or just simply consciousness. Our inner secret selves are revealed through the recycled material that comes originally from the stars. This becomes an intriguing reflection when we struggle to find words and thoughts to answer the question 'Who am I?'

Growing Older & Finding Creative Activity

Getting older is not always easy, and to a greater or lesser extent we all have our grumpy moments. 'Once I was "Little Rosie" – soon I shall be "The Old Woman",' laments the middle-aged Marschallin in Strauss' opera *Der Rosenkavalier*. But the realization that we are part of a creative recycling process gives us a new perspective, helping us to see that old age is itself a proper part of our life's trajectory; we can take it in our stride, celebrating each day as it comes. This ageing process is no accident but it is how we are made, to live transitory lives on earth, making room for the next generation. Galileo himself, centuries before the theory of evolution explained the importance of generation replacing generation, was critical of the values of those academics who, with Aristotle, exalted incorruptibility; 'These individuals do not reflect that if man was immortal, they themselves would never have come into the world.'[1]

An old historian friend of mine, a retired cleric in his late nineties, when I asked what he was reading, told me with an amused chuckle, 'I'm reading some books I wrote in my youth – and discovering all sorts of things I never knew I knew!' Galileo had a similar experience with old age, though his response was perhaps not so light-hearted; he wrote to a friend, 'I find how much old age lessens the vividness and speed of my thinking, as I struggle to understand quite a lot of things I discovered and proved when I was younger.'[1]

People as Co-Creators

A key to understanding our lives as we grow older lies in the word *creative;* we have emerged from a creative process. The biblical idea that men and women are all made in the image of God has intrigued the readers of Genesis for thousands of years. What is interesting is that the only thing revealed about God in this story is that he is creator of everything in heaven and earth. The implication then is that we too, made in this image, can be co-creators.

It is attested by many people, whatever their age, that they feel most themselves, most fulfilled and happy, when they are involved in some form of creative activity. This becomes particularly true for those who have retired from full-time employment. The parameters are wide and each of us will find individual ways to be creative – cooking for friends or family, painting, writing, volunteering, organizing, making friends, leavening our inner lives through meditation, disturbing the peace in matters of justice… The list is as long as the number of people on the planet.

Connections

We are not alone in the answers we find to the question 'Who are we?'; and we cannot separate ourselves from all that is around us. The answers must embrace all life forms; they belong equally to the nightingale and the house sparrow, to the minnow and the porpoise, the nettle and the delphinium. We are all part of the same emerging process of life on Earth. When I have travelled home on a late-night London underground line, I have never minded waiting for the train, because then I had time to watch for the tiny mice that scuttled about beneath the lines, foraging for crumbs of food. Four-legged mammals grown from the same material as I am, with fingers and toes just like me but living in a world so different from mine; and yet I only have to think back one hundred million years and their grandparents were my grandparents.

CHAPTER THREE

THE TROUBLING SIZE OF THE UNIVERSE

The unimaginable size of the universe can be troubling – the great distances to the stars, the mind-numbing numbers involved, the awe-inspiring depths of empty space, dark and unknown. But in the words of Cambridge astronomer Anthony Hewish, whose work has focused on the radio emissions of distant stars, 'Without all this vastness, we would not be here'. We may feel small in the face of the cosmos but there are ways to understand and cope with that.

THE VAST UNBOUNDED DEEP

We need to find a way of thinking about this vast cosmic environment we inhabit, the blizzards of stars that fill this ancient universe, the voids of empty space beyond anything we can hope to imagine. Alien as it may all seem, we can begin to feel that this is our home.

LET US STEP OUTSIDE to spend some time with the Milky Way. Even in a city, this might be possible – I have sometimes glimpsed that faint ribbon of light, running right down the sky to the horizon, from my back garden when I lived in London's Hammersmith; hard to make out, but definitely there. It is much better, however, to view it from the deeper darkness of the countryside; best still from somewhere like the outback in Australia or any remote spot, such as a desert, where light pollution has not yet penetrated.

The Milky Way is always above us somewhere in the night sky, although its position and angle are continually changing, either running directly overhead, or lying along the horizon, depending on the time of year. If you followed it around the world you would find that it completely circles the heavens, which is why part of it is visible at all times of the night. The people of Mongolia, drawing perhaps on earlier Babylonian mythology, used to refer to it as the Heavenly Seam, believing that it followed the line where two hemispherical parts of heaven are sewn together to make a perfect sphere.

The Milky Way in Myth & Legend

Ancient Chinese legend has it that the Milky Way, the *Silver* or *Heavenly River*, is a stream in the heavens separating two lovers, the cowherd Niulang and the weaver girl Zhinu. There are many variations of the story but in essence they all tell how Zhinu, daughter of a goddess, had offended heaven by falling in love with a lowly mortal, the cowherd, and marrying beneath her. Niulang and Zhinu were banished from Earth by her mother or another angry goddess to become two bright stars in the sky – respectively, Altair in the constellation of Aquila and Vega in the constellation of Lyra.

A traditional Chinese festival, Qixi, particularly popular among young girls, is celebrated annually on the seventh day of the seventh lunar month, when a flock of friendly magpies is said to form a bridge across the *Silver River* via the star Deneb in the constellation of Cygnus, so that the lovers may be together again. The three stars – Vega, Altair and Deneb – create what is often known in the West as the Summer Triangle, high overhead on northern summer nights.

Life, death, love and immortality are themes that dominate the world's mythology associated with the Milky Way. In many legends it is the source of a great river, such as the Nile in Egypt or the Yellow River of China; and many believed it to be the pathway taken by ghosts of the dead to another world. For Norsemen, it was the route followed by departed warriors as they travelled to Valhalla. In Hindu myth it is the celestial

As I get older, it is the familiarity of the Milky Way that I find so arresting.

river from which the gods seized the elixir of life, the gift of immortality; whereas the Chinese believed that if you followed the Yellow River upstream far enough, you would come to the *Heavenly River* on whose banks grow fabulous peaches that confer eternal life on anyone who eats them.

A Familiar Sight

How many of our ancestors have gazed, with us, at that milky river of light running among the stars (for it has not altered its path or shape in recorded history) and wondered wistfully what was to become of them after death? Would they leave their families behind at the funeral service and go to some heavenly place?

As I get older, it is the familiarity of the Milky Way that I find so arresting; it bridges my life from early childhood, when my parents first pointed it out to me in 1945 in the dark night sky of Cumbria, up to the present day when I can enjoy looking up on relaxed evenings, strolling in the garden with my wife, Ros, in East Sussex. I can still see, in my mind's eye, that first sight I had of it from the vicarage garden in Eskdale, silent and serene, meandering among the stars down to the horizon where it was blocked by the dark bulk of Birker Moor to the south. It is unchanged; unchanged even since before the first story tellers wove it into their legends – and will remain unchanged while innumerable generations of grandchildren come and go.

Familiarity is one of the great comforts of ageing. My body grows older by the day and I tire more easily; but my inner self, the more important me, remains the same. It is both pleasing and soothing to find that the Milky Way stays with me, unaltered, in my lifetime. Wordsworth's phrase 'intimations of immortality' comes naturally to mind as I contemplate

The Starry Messenger

When Galileo turned his telescope upon the Milky Way in 1610, he must have been just as astonished by what he saw as he had been when viewing for the first time the four moons orbiting Jupiter. The invention of the telescope has to be one of the great high points in the history of astronomy – and of humanity. Galileo's instrument magnified a mere thirty-three diameters and was no better than the good pair of Zeiss binoculars that I use for bird-watching today. And yet with this poor instrument he was to make another great discovery. He observed that the Milky Way resolved itself into myriads of stars too faint to be seen individually with the naked eye.

this ancient river of light among the stars. My life may be brief here on earth, but in a timeless moment of meditation on something as old as the Milky Way, its brevity seems unimportant – irrelevant even.

For every star visible to the unaided eye, Galileo's telescope revealed ten more. It was these new distant stars and the tracts of space between them that caught the imagination of the ordinary reader of *The Starry Messenger,* the brief pamphlet he wrote to publicize his discoveries that year. In the star fields of the Milky Way, Galileo had discovered the 'vast unbounded deep' of space. Those infinite tracts of emptiness *between* the stars were unthinkable; contemplation of these great voids shook and thrilled his readers. The sheer size of the universe was beginning to put a strain on the imaginations of the most mentally adventurous. Galileo's name was guaranteed a stellar place in history.

Notes to Grandchildren

• Locate the star Vega in the constellation of Lyra – it is high overhead during the northern summer. This is the first star I learned to identify. Our world, with the Sun and other planets, is ceaselessly drifting through space towards Vega at 20 kilometres (12.5 miles) per second.

Early Problems with Size & Distance

We are not the first to find it difficult to think about the size of the universe. Early Greek astronomers were aware of some problems. Aristotle had already observed, in the fourth century BC, that the surface of the world was curved: ships sail *over* the horizon; stars in the northern heavens sink lower in the sky as you travel south and new constellations appear in the southern skies. These observations supported the Babylonian observation that the world must be round because of the shadow it casts upon the Moon during a lunar eclipse.

Another Greek scholar, Eratosthenes, had calculated the diameter of the world with extraordinary accuracy in the second century BC. He observed that the midday sun shining straight down a well in southern Egypt was seven degrees from doing so in northern Egypt; knowing the distance between the two places, he was able to calculate the circumference of the whole earth. It was this newly measured size of the Earth that gave early astronomers a problem.

If the Sun and stars orbited the Earth as they then believed, they should be much larger overhead than they are when near the horizon. The branches of a copse of trees, for example, will fill the sky if we stroll among them; but seen on the horizon they appear as no more than a small clump. Intuition and experience would suggest that the Sun and stars should get smaller as they head for the horizon, the constellations shrinking in size, as would a skein of geese. But as the dimensions of

Sun and stars remained unaltered (a fact we can check for ourselves) whether over the horizon or high overhead, they could only conclude that they must be *very* far away, further off than would fit neatly into the image they had of the cosmos.

Despite these observations, the Greeks remained wedded to an Earth-centred universe, a view reinforced by the great astronomer Ptolemy, who constructed an imagined model of the universe in which the Sun, Moon and planets were fixed to invisible crystal spheres as they pursued their different orbits around the Earth. The stars were attached to the furthest and outermost sphere, revolving about us like the outer skin of a glass onion. This Ptolemaic system ruled and hindered the minds of curious thinkers for one thousand four hundred years. It was unwieldy; the outer sphere of stars, for instance, was already suspected to be so far away that it would have to spin at an unbelievable speed to complete a revolution in just twenty-four hours. But no one came up with an alternative until Copernicus with his mathematics and Galileo with his telescope shattered the crystal spheres completely.

The stars were attached to the furthest and outermost sphere, revolving about us like the outer skin of a glass onion

CONTEMPLATING THE MILKY WAY

◆

Let us gaze up at the Milky Way. Allow time for the eyes to adjust
to the dark; and for our minds and hearts to come into the present
moment. We are looking at the galaxy. For this we need imagination
— not to dream up fantasies, but to cope with all that astronomers
tell about it.

WHAT GALILEO FIRST OBSERVED was only a hint of the
vast depths of space to be discovered with larger
instruments. The galaxy (the word is formed from the ancient
Greek word *gala*, meaning milk) is composed of over a thousand million stars — of which our own Sun is an average-sized
star — in the shape of a flat disc, turning slowly like a great
wheel. But most of it is empty space; if one were to represent
each of its stars by a grain of sugar then the grains would, on
the same scale, have to be 3 kilometres (1.9 miles) apart. At
this point, a sort of mental vertigo infects our imagination.

The Milky Way turns: but in all its history it has turned
around its centre only about twenty times, the stars taking a
quarter of a million years to make the circuit just once,
a period of time that dwarfs the era in which human beings
have inhabited the earth. The very best time to observe it is on
a summer night in the northern hemisphere (winter in the
southern hemisphere). The star clouds in the constellation of
Sagittarius near the southern horizon are the brightest and

The Black Hole

There is an object lurking in the star clouds of Sagittarius that completely defies our imagination: it is a Black Hole. Many other galaxies sport one at their centres. To call such an exotic object a Black Hole is really a misnomer: nothing could be more different from 'hole' as it is the densest creature in the stellar zoo. A black hole of this sort is a massive collapsed star; gravity has overcome all other forces, drawing all its material into a knot so dense that light cannot escape and so to the astronomer it is invisible. The Black Hole in Sagittarius is the mass of a billion suns (and, fortunately for the solar system, twenty-seven thousand light years distant). Astronomers using radio telescopes are able to track the orbits of stars close to this monster; stars that will eventually be torn apart and drawn into its invisible maw.

most dramatic, often noticed by northerners when taking a summer holiday by the Mediterranean. Through binoculars, this part of the Milky Way is even richer in stars. The reason is simple; we are now looking towards the heart of the galaxy, around which our Sun circles slowly. Slowly? Actually, we fly with our Sun, and its other attendant planets in this greater galactic orbit, at 250 kilometres (155 miles) per second. Our planet is already a spaceship carrying us through the universe far faster than anything possible using current technology.

Cygnus the Swan

Another beautiful patch of the Milky Way lies overhead if you live in European and North American latitudes; this is where it runs through Cygnus the Swan, a constellation easy to identify because the stars are arranged in the shape of a cross or a long-necked swan flying down the Milky Way towards Sagittarius. The bright star Vega, the 'weaver girl' of Chinese legend, shines west of Cygnus. Her lover, Altair, shines further south to the east. Oh, for the bridge of magpies!

In Cygnus there appears to be a hole in the sky, a dark rift in the Milky Way. In fact, it is not an absence of stars at all, for they are all there, but obscured to our eyes by a vast cloud of interstellar dust and gas. And it was from such a cloud that our Sun and planets were born four and a half billion years ago; it was a cloud like this, containing the sprinkling of atoms forged in older suns, that provided all the material needed to evolve life on Earth and build our brains and bodies.

Small but Significant

By contemplating the Milky Way, we have come full circle and returned to the theme of the last chapter – that we are made from star dust. This fact must have something to tell us about the size of the universe and our own apparent insignificance.

The size of the galaxy can be intimidating. Our own Sun is nothing special but an insignificant star far out from the galactic centre. And to make matters worse (or certainly more awe-inspiring), we now know that our galaxy is one among a thousand million others spread out through the void. We may be tempted to feel that we are nothing and valueless.

Yet, despite feeling small, we belong to this universe in a very intimate way. Stars had to burn and die for the atoms that build us to be forged, and then released into the clouds of interstellar space before our own solar system could be formed. Without the universe being vast and ancient, populated with nuclear furnaces in the hearts of massive suns cooking up the atoms of carbon, oxygen and so forth, we could not be here; these are the pre-conditions that are essential for life on Earth to evolve. It takes a universe of this size to make people.

Since when has bigger meant better? It is a misreading of the science to conclude that we have no significance simply because we are small compared to the rest of the cosmos. We can say with confidence that this is a universe designed to create conscious life and people, whether by God, or simply by the laws of physics, or by both – depending on our belief. However small we may be compared to the dimensions of our galaxy, the very size of the universe we inhabit gives us extraordinary value. We, and the richly emerging ecosystem that we share, are what it is all about.

How Did the Galaxy Come to Be?

Was this whole universe of galaxies, of Milky Way systems, created or did it just happen? Human curiosity finds it hard not to ask the question. Who or what creates our world, the immense realms of emptiness, the myriads of stars both in and beyond the Milky Way? Is God the 'Creator of Heaven and Earth' as stated in the Christian creed? Or is the whole cosmos merely a consequence of the laws of physics – and, if so, then how are we to account for the laws of physics themselves, so creative in their manifestation? Buddhism sets the whole question to one side as not immediately helpful in our quest for enlightenment. Some people will find it valuable to live without answers to the question of origins; others will find thoughts of a purposeful loving creator as more helpful.

Personally, I still, after a long life of alternating faith and doubt, believe in God. Not in 'a' God, a separate being sitting somehow above us, but in a creative loving power within whom we live and move and have our being – the underlying cause of all that is. I cannot prove that my view is right – but it continues, sometimes against all the odds, to *feel* right. It is a mystery that I am happy to live with, and find very easy, particularly when alone, to address as 'Lord', as in 'Into thy hands, Oh Lord, I commend my spirit' as I prepare for sleep. It seems a natural thing to say after standing out under the stars, as I nightly let go of consciousness.

CHAPTER FOUR

MARS,
THE BRINGER
OF WAR

*It would be interesting to know how
we would think about the heavens above us if we
did not have access to four hundred years of scientific
enquiry, to the thousands of books and TV programmes
dedicated to the subject. A few years ago I had the
privilege of finding out, by spending an evening by a
camp fire in the Laikipia region of Kenya with an old
Samburu herdsman, revered in his community as a Star
Man. Our discussion ranged from Mars to shooting
stars. I also discovered some truths about old age.*

NOMADIC STORY TELLERS
& A STAR MAN

◆

Leparia was an elder in his community, a gentle presence with twinkling eyes; slightly built with a respectful silence in his face, something I had noticed in other tribal elders. He accepted life gratefully as it came to him and lived it at the walking pace of a herdsman. Leparia was mindfulness personified.

THE STAR MAN HAD WALKED FOR TWO DAYS to attend our meeting in the bush; he had learned by word of mouth that I wanted to talk with him. A message from my friend Sveva had brought him to where I was staying at Ol Ari Nyiro on the edge of the African Rift Valley. I was assisting Sveva at the time with something called the Four Generations Project[4], a programme to be used in schools to inspire children to question their grandparents and great-grandparents about what they remembered from their childhoods – what plants could be used medicinally, what myths and legends they recalled being told, what stories they could recollect from the history of their tribe. It is important to recognize the wisdom of past generations and to record these things before they are forgotten. Valuable lessons and truths held only in human memories can be lost for ever.

As darkness fell that evening, Leparia opened an old bag and unfolded a goatskin cloak, bordered with camel's hair and

decorated with beads and cowry shells. He fastened the cloak around his shoulders, explaining that he always wore it when watching or talking about the stars. He was putting himself in 'the right place' for contemplating the heavens.

We sat in the dark by the embers of a fire; two old men discussing what they had learned in their lives about the sky. Sveva was there, and an interpreter – though strangely I remember nothing of the interpreter, who must have been very good, because, as I recall the evening, my discussions with Leparia were direct and unmediated. A herd of elephants walked silently by, crossing the clearing not more than two hundred yards away; a lion roared in the distance, prowling about, 'seeking whom he may devour'.

Leparia pointed to the constellation of Ursa Major, the Great Bear, popularly known to us as the Plough or the Big Dipper. It was an elephant to him – the four stars in a rectangle marked the feet of the beast, and the three stars that we see as the handle of the plough represented three hunters following the elephant. In northern latitudes where I grew up, the Plough never sets, but turns throughout the night around Polaris, the Pole Star. In Kenya, which is on the equator, the Plough dips beneath the northern horizon. For Leparia, the three hunters were chasing the elephant down into the bush, only to emerge again later in the year, still chasing, on their celestial merry-go-round. The patterns we see are mostly imposed by our minds.

Shared Fascination

We exchanged stories about how we had first become interested in the night sky; both of us, it seemed, had been intrigued by the sudden and unexpected appearance and disappearance of shooting stars as they flashed across the sky. In Samburu story-telling, shooting stars are supposed to be sent by God to pierce the ground and produce springs of water for his people. Leparia, driven by a spirit of curiosity, had made many enquiries throughout his life about bright shooting stars he had seen while tending his cattle. After walking many miles on many occasions, however, he found no evidence that they had landed and made holes in the ground – so he was inclined to disbelieve this tradition. Ever since being a little boy, he had looked after the family's cattle and slept out under the stars to keep an eye on the herd. A memory amused him and he told me how one night he had become so occupied with gazing up at the sky, trying to learn its star patterns, that his cows had all wandered off into the bush!

Mars, the brightest object in the sky that evening, was high above us and glowing red through the thin branches of a yellow fever tree; I was eager to know what Leparia thought of the Red Planet. He told me that by its rising and varying brightness he learned about the likelihood and direction of war, and was delighted when I explained that because of its angry colour the Romans had named it Mars after their god of war. I am not sure what he knew about the war then being

waged against Saddam Hussein in Iraq, but he swung his arm in that direction and nodded sadly.

A Samburu Legend

Later that night the bright and pearly cream-coloured planet Jupiter rose above the bush to the east, very unlike the fiery red of Mars, which by now was heading down to the western horizon. And I learned an extraordinary story. According to Samburu legend, the tribe's ancestors had been lowered to Earth on a rope, along with their cattle, from Jupiter, which they called 'The Crossing Star' – a name it had attained to distinguish it from Venus, also very bright (Venus orbits closer than us to the Sun and is only ever seen following the Sun down after sunset as the Evening Star, or rising before it in the morning as the Morning Star; it never crosses the sky during the night, as does Jupiter). These ancestors, I was surprised to discover, had landed on a mountain called Mount Sinai. All was good and peaceful, until one of them had upset God by asking for a yellow cow (a golden calf?). God was angry with them and cut the rope linking him to the tribe. Their life was disturbed by this and they then had to flee from Sinai, which they did by passing through a sea whose waves parted before them. They finally settled near a new sacred mountain, Mount Nyiro, in what is now northern Kenya.

Good stories have their own power and it seems that in this case there are biblical echoes of the early wanderings of the

Israelites, in their tribal days. Somehow these tales have found their way into Samburu legend.

Exchanging Blessings

Leparia was curious about my own astronomical knowledge; he welcomed new thoughts and was a great example of someone for whom old age offered no hindrance to the acceptance of new ideas. He wanted to know how I interpreted solar eclipses. For the Samburu, an eclipse is an indication that the Sun's light is fading and losing its power, a warning of God's anger; but it seemed to the Star Man that something was blocking the light. When I explained what I had learned about the Moon and its orbit, and that eclipses always occurred when the old Moon drew near to the Sun, he beamed with delight and said that he had always suspected it! An open and enquiring mind is not the prerogative of the young.

Before turning in for the night, we asked Leparia for his blessing; we were sitting on logs and he turned us to the north-east and Mount Nyiro. We held out our upturned hands to draw ourselves closer to God while Leparia breathed over us and blessed us with his fly whisk.

Then he asked for my blessing as a Christian priest – and I was much moved.

By the time I awoke the next morning, Leparia had already departed, walking silently back through the bush to his cattle and his family. I had learned a great deal when speaking to

him, and not simply about tribal legends and beliefs. He had grown old without any of the 'success' or accumulation of possessions or wealth that we seem to crave in Western society – and he looked back with a wonderful smile on a long life. He accepted his lot as a nomadic herdsman, a life enriched with a love of the stars, with unquestioning pleasure. He believed with gratitude that God had blessed him.

Mindfulness Personified

I think of Leparia as 'mindfulness personified', because while talking with him, I felt that he had a calm inner stillness that gave him the security and confidence to entertain new ideas. He had conducted his own limited research into shooting stars and had questioned the Samburu beliefs about eclipses; he looked at the skies with fond respect and an open mind; his heart was peaceful. Curiosity in his old age came quite naturally to him.

I have noticed this quiet acceptance of old age, with its physical limitations, in the sun-wrinkled faces of many ageing tribal people in Kenya. Bare-footed, seated perhaps on a rough log and often displaying a toothless grin, they seem, in living in the present moment, to have everything. How different from the eminently successful medical practitioner I once knew, with a high public profile, who suffered from depression and bitterness in old age because, as his wife explained, he felt his life had been a failure.

THE BAFFLING ORBIT OF MARS

◆

Mars, which Leparia and I had observed from our camp fire, is well worth looking for and pondering over. It was known to early Greek astronomers as one of the five 'wandering stars', and moved through the constellations of the zodiac in a perplexing way.

M ARS IS RED BECAUSE OF THE RUSTINESS of its deserts, whose dust storms can sometimes engulf the whole planet, and very bright at its nearest to Earth in a midnight sky. In many respects, it is an Earth-like world, one that astronauts of the near future will surely visit (I am learning to accept now, as I get older, that this will probably not be in my lifetime!). The planet's current position among the stars can be found by consulting any astronomical calendar, either in a newspaper or on the internet.

Mars travels fast in its orbit around the Sun compared to, say, Jupiter, which takes twelve Earth-years to complete just one circuit (a Jupiter-year), moving in that time through each sign of the zodiac. Mars has a smaller orbit, although larger than the Earth's, and completes a single orbit in just under two Earth-years. It is further out from the Sun than we are, and we keep catching it up on our inner faster track and overtaking it. This simple fact created many problems for early astronomers, because they were hampered by the belief that the Earth was stationary.

Retrograde Motion

If you locate Mars in the night sky and become struck by its beauty, and find yourself checking it out during the next few weeks and months, you might note something strange. It quickly becomes apparent that it moves against the background stars of the zodiacal constellation it occupies, moving to the east most of the time as it pursues its orbit around the Sun. Then, slowing down, it comes to a stop and reverses its direction for a few weeks, before returning to its normal easterly progress. Mars seems to be performing a sedate dance; advancing forward then taking a few steps back before stepping forward once more. With immense patience, the planets Jupiter and Saturn can be seen to be acting in a similar way, though more slowly. This presented a problem for astronomers in the past.

Copernicus, with his mathematics, and Galileo later supporting him with his telescope, found the solution. Since the days of Aristotle in the fourth century BC, people had been wedded to a number of mistaken ideas about the world. Questioning these ideas was hard because Aristotle had become so admired in the Middle Ages that he was known simply as 'The Philosopher', and not to be doubted; he was adopted as an authority on the natural world by the Roman Catholic Church. He created the world view that dominated the minds of scholars for generations. It was Aristotle who asserted, for example, that heavy objects fall faster than light objects – and no one thought to question the fact until Galileo suggested testing the theory by dropping objects of differing weight from the top of the leaning tower of Pisa. Aristotelian followers of 'The Philosopher' were furious; to question his teachings was impertinence of the highest order.

The Celestial Dance

Aristotle believed that the Earth was at the centre of the universe, but was a corrupt and imperfect place, whereas everything beyond the orbit of the Moon was perfect. Ptolemy, his astronomical follower two centuries later, created the rigid model of the universe as a nesting set of crystal spheres ranging out from the Moon to the sphere of stars. But Mars and the other outer planets behaved strangely in their celestial dance 'around' the Earth; four steps forward then two steps back.... The only way Ptolemy could accommodate this behaviour was to have them spinning on little extra cycles (the circle being perfect in Aristotle's philosophy) as they orbited the Earth: an immensely complicated arrangement, because it was constrained by Aristotelian views of perfection.

Copernicus and Galileo smashed the imaginary crystal spheres and gave us a new way of viewing the world, with the Sun at the centre of the solar system. Then Kepler, an admirer and contemporary of Galileo, revealed that the orbits are not 'perfect' circles at all, as Aristotle had taught they should be, but are ellipses. People began to question what we mean by

perfection anyway – why should an ellipse be any less perfect than a circle? We now know from the work of Galileo and company that the apparent dance of the outer planets can be simply explained as being due to our moving standpoint on Earth as we overtake them on our inner faster track while we orbit the Sun in twelve months.

GALILEO OFFENDS THE CHURCH

◆

Galileo found himself in trouble with reactionaries in the Church for supporting the Copernican view of the world – that it turned on its axis daily and moved through space around the Sun. He was also in trouble for destroying the distinction between Heaven and Earth.

THROUGH HIS TELESCOPE, GALILEO had seen the surface of the Moon and observed that it was a world like this one, not at all perfect but covered with deserts and mountains and deep valleys. He had also viewed the Sun through mist and discovered (something Chinese astronomers had observed over a millennium earlier) that the Sun had spots on its surface, which came and went. The heavens above were not as perfect and unchanging as had been thought.

Many people welcomed Galileo's discoveries and there were some who even argued that he had done mankind a service. In the Aristotelian world system adopted by the Church, humanity lived near the bottom of creation – only one floor up from the pit of hell, so vividly described by Dante. Far from demoting humanity from its important place at the centre of everything, as many feared he was doing, he had helped set Earth free to fly through the heavens, dissolving the distinction between perfection and imperfection, between Heaven and Earth.

The Inquisition

Galileo had a tough time with the Inquisition, a corrupt growth within the judicial system of the medieval Christian Church, beginning in the thirteenth century. It was founded to combat heresy – any beliefs that ran counter to orthodox teaching – and resorted, in imposing its will, to inhuman and thoroughly unchristian practices. It is often said that power corrupts; religious institutions are not immune to this failing. The Inquisition ruled through fear, adopting horrendous methods of bullying. Galileo must have been made deeply anxious when the Inquisition burned the renegade monk Giordano Bruno at the stake for holding views deemed unacceptable – that the Earth moved and that the starry heavens might be peopled with other inhabited worlds.

Ironically, the fear that the Inquisition used to control Catholic believers was itself inspired by fear – the fear of losing control, every bit as inhuman and dishonourable as the 'control freak' who beats his wife and children. The ruling powers in the Church had lost much of northern Europe to

Letting Go

When we centre ourselves in the practice of mindfulness, we are letting go of the complex world of regrets, worries, anxieties, fears, needs, wants and so forth and simply focusing on the present moment, letting ourselves become aware of our bodies and of our breathing. There is a wonderful security to be found in this liberating practice, a security that will give us the power to think helpfully about the world we inhabit. We then might ask ourselves: do we impose any ideas of the world and its workings upon other people that we could do well to rethink? Are we in the grip of a world view that we have not really questioned? Have we allowed events of the past to poison the present moment? As we age, it might be good to sort some of these things out.

Protestant sects; and now with Galileo they were becoming seriously disturbed by the direction taken by Aristotelian philosophy, that backbone of Christian theology. Aristotle, with his 'common sense' view of the world, supported and promoted by so many scholars of the age, was being questioned, undermined and even rejected. Fear of losing power and control caused the Church to harden up in a terrible way. Heresy became punishable by death.

Unlike my friend Leparia, the personification of mindfulness, those in power in the seventeenth-century Church were not able to take on board new ideas that altered their view of the world, or relax with a smile and see things differently. Many people did show curiosity and questioning interest in what Galileo saw through his telescope, but they were frightened by the system, and by what today we might call the 'thought police'.

Last Years

Galileo did not make things easy for himself. He had many admirers and lots of scholars of his day agreed with him, but he was a difficult, proud man who ridiculed his enemies with a sharp wit – not the best way to make friends. He could have kept a lower profile and it has been argued that he brought the trial for heresy down upon himself. Galileo put the authorities in a difficult position. In 1632 he wrote *Dialogue on the Great Systems of the World,* the title itself having been proposed by his friend Barberini, who was about to become Pope Urban VIII. Tactlessly, Galileo cast his *Dialogue* as a debate between the brilliant savant Salviati, his own mouthpiece, and Simplicio, a good-humoured simpleton who represented the views of the old-fashioned Church scholars and the Inquisition. It didn't go down well with the Pope.

Fortunately, the authorities handled him more gently than they had Bruno: he was committed to house arrest, told not

to promulgate his views and ordered to recite the seven peni-
tential psalms once a week. His daughter, Sister Maria Celeste,
took up the latter task by reciting them for him in her con-
vent. He continued writing and safely remained in contact by
letter with followers in the Protestant north of Europe. He
remained a good Catholic Christian to his dying day, at log-
gerheads with authority but not with the gospel.

Notes to Grandchildren

• Do not allow past regrets to rule your life; the episodes
you regret are simply part of the track you followed that
brought you to this present moment. Live *now* with happiness.

• Never ever bully – physically, emotionally or verbally.
Beware of being drawn into a bullying situation; even the
Christian Church was corrupted by this horrible behaviour in
medieval times.

• Be grateful all the time for the good things of life; for the
day, for your breath, for your digestion and your health, for
love of friends and family. This is not a duty (like being told to
say 'thank you' by a grumpy grandpa); you will find that being
grateful is itself a joy and a pleasure.

• Never let yourself worry about, or be upset by, growing
older. It is a natural process.

CHAPTER FIVE

TIME TUNNELS
& ETERNITY

*It rarely occurs to us — if ever — to think of
astronomers as historians. The light and radio waves
that come to their telescopes from deep space, carrying
with them so much information about the way the stars
are moving, their chemical makeup and temperature,
take time to reach Earth. As we let our minds
explore the sky on a dark night, we find ourselves
peering back into a past that pre-dates us,
in some cases by millions of years.*

EXCITE YOUR CURIOSITY

◆

*The absurdly misguided warning to children that 'curiosity killed
the cat' should be banned from folk memory. 'Be careful...' certainly, and then '...but let your curiosity run and run.' Curiosity is
one of the distinctive features of our humanity – it makes us creative
and inventive; it gives us deep pleasure, whatever our age.*

FOUR LEATHER-BOUND VOLUMES of an eighteenth-century
work called *Nature Displayed* by Noël Antoine Pluche
(published 1732) have been resting on my shelf for the past
forty years. I am very fond of them and suspect I love their
simply tooled bindings as much as I do their contents. Held in
the hand, there is something solid and pleasing about them.
Nature Displayed was a product of the French Enlightenment,
its original title being *Spectacle de la Nature*. Mine is an English
edition, published by Pemberton in Fleet Street in 1739. The
complete title is typical of its age and worth savouring: '*Nature
Displayed, being Discourses on such particulars of Natural History as
were thought most proper to Excite the Curiosity and Form the Minds
of Youth.*' What a lovely aspiration that contains!

But curiosity is not, emphatically, the privilege of youth.
Many writers on the subject of old age have expressed the
view that it is a continuing curiosity about the world that
keeps them feeling young. Those of us who are getting older
need to be alert to this witness and to remember what a

delight it is to be in conversation with a youthful mind sparkling in an old body. One of the great features of ageing, and retirement from full-time employment, is that it opens up so many opportunities to explore those interests that tickle the mind with curiosity.

Gentlemanly Facts

It was not just youth, in the Enlightenment of the eighteenth century, whose minds could be woken to all the new wonders of the world then being revealed by science – Erasmus Darwin, grandfather of Charles, on founding the Derby Philosophical Society in 1783, announced that his society would seek 'gentlemanly facts'. (I wonder if there was a subcommittee appointed to deal with and possibly suppress those discoveries that were less than gentlemanly – and what they might be. Perhaps only senior citizens would be allowed access to these savoury delights!)

My father had his own version of 'gentlemanly facts' which he called 'useless information'; it kept him interested in life, along with his daily crossword, curious about the world up to the day he died. 'Useless information' found its way into his sermons and into mealtime conversation; it meant any

It is a continuing curiosity about the world that keeps them feeling young.

interesting fact whose value lay solely in sparking some sense of wonder, fascinating in itself. A week before he died, at eighty-two (young, I now think), I was sitting by his bed and told him of something I had just read in the *New Scientist* about the dispersal of willow-herb seeds. 'Really; is that so?' he said, sounding intrigued; and I could see from his face that he was storing the information up to tell someone else.

SEEKING DARKNESS

◆

One of God's greatest gifts to humanity, according to Volume 4 of Nature Displayed, was the gift of darkness; with the fall of night, the farm labourer and his wife could lay down their weary limbs and take their rest.

THE FOUR VOLUMES OF *Nature Displayed* cover all that was then known about the natural world, from sea urchins to stars, while expressing the view that God in his benevolence has blessed us with wonderful things. He has, for example, given us the night: 'Night, indeed, in covering all Objects with Darkness, obliges Man to cease from his Works.' Some might disapprove today of such an anthropomorphic view of the world; I find it charming, if dated.

God in his care and compassion, we read, has even thought to bring on the darkness slowly from sundown to nightfall, so as not to catch us unawares but allow us time to finish

whatever task is in hand. A universal silence then follows: 'During all the Time of Man's Repose, Night, for his sake, hushes every Noise, keeps off all glaring Lights, and whatever might strongly affect him. It, indeed, suffers a few Animals, whose grim Aspect might scare him while he is at work, to go forth under favour of its Darkness, and silently seek their Food in the abandoned Fields.' A reading of this lovely flowing sentiment can be somewhat hesitant, since the early printers often used 'f' in place of 's'.

While we may not go along with the delightful details of this natural theology and its vision of a hands-on God designing every element of the created world with humanity in mind, we do seem to have lost, in our more modern world, any sense of the 'goodness' of the dark. We are missing something if we cannot find a place for true darkness in our lives.

A Place of Special Delight

One of the darkest places I know in England is the Wasdale Valley in Cumbria, hosting the country's deepest lake, Wastwater. My brother Inigo lives there, and to walk home with him from the pub down a country lane without street lights is a special delight. A stream gurgles by the track and overhead the branches of alder, hazel and ash are dark silhouettes against the night sky; a high mountain ridge, the Wastwater Screes, looms to the south. We have to look up at the sky to keep on the path, or to catch the faint light reflected ahead of us in puddles. I have often stopped on this lane to smell the night air and perhaps catch the scent of newly mown grass from the hayfield. I stand by a field gate next to a drystone wall. An owl hoots from the oak woods nearby and a farm dog barks in the distance. The sounds of night have their own delicious quality, gentle and arresting.

It may be a cloudy night – it often is – but waiting can bring its own rewards. There is nothing more beautiful to my mind than to watch a parting of the clouds and to see the stars then revealed, clear and fresh as though washed by rain. As the clouds draw back, the constellations become recognizable, appearing brighter than usual. Sometimes they sparkle with such intimate clarity in their velvet darkness, it seems one could almost touch them.

But they are, in fact, so far off that the distances are worth pondering while we stand and stare by that field gate. Galileo's admiring contemporary, Kepler (he who discovered the laws of planetary motion), believed that we see the stars exactly as they are, now, instantaneously in the present moment. He believed that the speed of light was infinite, so that there was no time lag between the light leaving the star and entering our eyes. Galileo disagreed.

The Speed of Light

Galileo believed that just as it takes sound time to travel across a field – observed, for instance, when the sight of a

woodman chopping a tree is followed by the delayed sound of the strike – so light must have its own measurable speed. Realizing that it must be very fast, he nevertheless tried to measure it. He set up an experiment to prove his theory by using shuttered lanterns on neighbouring hilltops; Galileo was on one hill with an assistant stationed over a mile away on another. He flashed a signal from his shuttered lantern and watched to see how long it took the assistant to flash him back. But the response time of the assistant, however bright and quick off the mark, was no match for the speed of light. The measurements came to nothing.

Galileo's intuition was correct, however – light *does* take time to travel from place to place; but he would have been surprised at the actual speed. Measurements were refined in the nineteenth century so that we now know the speed of light to be 300,000 kilometres / 186,000 miles (or over seven times round the world) per second. It is no wonder that Galileo and his helper were unable to gain any grasp of the actual figure. It is the top speed, beyond which nothing in the universe travels faster.

What the Speed of Light Means To Us

For us, quietly watching stars in the night sky, the speed of light has some fascinating consequences. Suppose it is December and we are looking up at Orion high over the equator. Bottom left of Orion (top right if viewing from Australia) is the bright star Sirius, its old Egyptian name meaning 'the scorcher'; seen from Earth, it is the brightest in our sky. Like the sound of the woodcutter's axe delayed when seen from the far side of a field, the light of Sirius is somewhat delayed by its speed, so we do not see it as it is now but as it was eight and a half years ago. What we see in our present moment is something happening eight and a half years in our past. What were we doing then?

To try to get some idea of what this means, just consider that the light reaching us from the Moon, perhaps even now in the sky as we see Sirius, takes just one and a quarter seconds to cover the 384,000 kilometres (240,000 miles) to reach us: light from the Sun, which set earlier, flashes across the 149 million kilometres (92 million miles) of space to illuminate our world in just eight and a half minutes. But from Sirius it takes eight and a half years; and so the star is said to be eight and a half light years away. The time light takes to travel from one place to another becomes a convenient and telling measure of distance, rather as I might say that I live only an hour from London, by train, rather than say it is 70 kilometres (43 miles) away.

Using light years as a measure of distance, we can then note that Betelgeuse in the shoulder of Orion is 450 light years away – we see it now as it was in the past, in the first Elizabethan era. The three stars of Orion's belt, true stellar giants, are seen even further back in history, for they shine to

Notes to Grandchildren

• Look for Altair in the constellation of Aquila, the most southerly star of the Summer Triangle and one of the closest to Earth. You see it as it was eleven years ago. What were you up to then?

---

us from hundreds of years before the days of William the Conqueror. Conversely, anyone living on a world in one of those solar systems in Orion's belt will see *us* as we were over a thousand years ago.

The Time Tunnel

Once aware of the time-delayed nature of the stars we see, we come to realize that when looking up at the sky, we observe nothing as it *is*, but are staring into the past and that each star is embedded in a different era of history. Every constellation becomes a 'time' tunnel through which we peer back into past ages. A neat example of this 'time tunnel' phenomenon is the northern hemisphere constellation of Cassiopeia; five bright stars form the shape of a 'W' and circle around the pole star during the night. The star at the top right, *Caph,* is forty-seven light years away, so I see it as it was when I was a young curate in Cirencester. The star at the top left of the 'W',

Segin, however, is 470 light years away and so I see it in the sixteenth century; it is ten times as far away as *Caph* and inhabiting a different period of history. Yet the 'W' of Cassiopeia appears to me a flat pattern on the sky – which is how the ancients thought the constellations to be, lights attached to the inside surface of a sphere. Somehow our new understanding of the heavens puts my meagre seventy-four years into perspective.

With patience and a simple star map, we can look even further back in time. The northern constellation of Andromeda contains a famous *nebula* (Latin for a cloud); to the naked eye it is no more than a faint patch of Milky Way-like light. Once detected, you may find it helpful to avert your stare slightly, shifting focus to one side – our eyes are more sensitive to light seen in peripheral vision, and the nebula will appear clearer as you look away from it. We now know it to be a massive neighbouring galaxy, a twin to our own Milky Way system, a collection of a hundred billion stars. What we see is from two and a half million years ago and is the furthest object to be visible to the unaided eye. We all of us had ancestors alive then; but what, I wonder, were they doing – and would we recognize them if we were to meet them?

Somehow our new understanding of the heavens puts my meagre seventy-four years into perspective.

Gazing to Infinity

When we gaze *between* the stars, how far can we see? How deep are the depths of space? The question as to whether the universe is infinite or not, going on and on for ever, has tantalized philosophers and astronomers down the ages. Equally problematic is the further question as to whether it has a beginning – or is eternal. Aristotle, that pre-Christian philosopher so revered by the medieval Church, believed in the infinity of the universe, stating that infinity 'is that which always has something beyond itself'. This caused something of a problem for many churchmen because they believed, from their Bible, that the universe was created 'in the beginning' by God, and is limited, finite in size.

Many Christian believers were heartened in the 1960s, when the 'Big Bang' theory of creation was advocated. It was then proposed that since the universe has been observed to be expanding, galaxies flying away from one another, we could trace all this motion back to an initial explosion, 13.7 billion years ago. Everything, it appeared, including space and time, had erupted from a single point, since dubbed a 'singularity'. The theory was hotly debated at the time by astrophysicists, with emotions running high in a manner that surprised non-scientists who assumed that science was a detached and cold subject. The idea of a definable beginning, however, chimed well with the belief that the universe was created by God. 'In the Beginning … God said "*Let there be light …*".'

The Big Bang Theory, now accepted by all astronomers to give a true account of the origins of space and time, did not, however, stop the debate. There is no scientific reason that this universe should not be one of a series of universes stretching back to infinity; expanding from a singularity only to collapse back aeons later into a singularity (dubbed the 'Big Crunch'), repeating the process for ever.

Back to The Here & Now

So, here we are by our gatepost in the dark, smelling the scent of newly mown grass from the field, gazing up between the stars, down time tunnels of history, to a beyond that evades our imagination. How far are we looking? We don't know. Is the universe eternal and has it always been here? We don't know. For those who believe in God as Creator, this presents no real problem, because God, always defined as eternal, could just as easily create continuously an eternal universe, as he could create one with a beginning, out of nothing. We face the present moment with this fascinating mystery. And there is nothing like trying to comprehend eternity for bringing us back into the here and now.

William Blake captured something of this in his *Auguries of Innocence;* 'To see a World in a Grain of Sand / Heaven in a Wild Flower / Hold Infinity in the palm of your hand / And Eternity in an hour.' Mindful attention to the present moment opens doors to eternity which is always with us.

TURNING TO THE FUTURE

◆

The future, unlike the past, offers exciting opportunities for change: it has not been predetermined. It is all too easy, as we get older, to fall into habits of thought and behaviour that close down our lives. But we can be creative with the time available to us.

AS WE MEDITATE UPON THE SKY, we are rooted in the here and now. Whichever way we look up, we are peering back into the past. The present moment only exists in our experience here about us, in our immediate surroundings – the hay field in darkness, the gatepost, and gravity gently pulling us to the ground.

But what of the future – does it also exist, like the past, but invisible to us? There is a strange imbalance in our lives between past and future, one known, and the other unknown. Not so very long ago, in the nineteenth century, scientists dreamed of being able, one day, to predict everything in the future of the universe with accuracy: they had only to apply the laws of physics. It might even be found, they thought, that similar laws were applicable to human behaviour, to our feelings and thoughts, so that what happens next in our lives is already predetermined, as surely as an egg rolling from a table will smash on the floor. But their thinking, then, had been infected by a false analogy, that the universe could be compared to a piece of well-oiled machinery.

If this rather depressing view of things had turned out to be true, we would have been reduced to being chemical robots lacking personal creativity or free will. However, there is good news – news that opens up the future wonderfully as we face it in the present moment.

Twentieth-century science discovered chaos theory and with it the principle of unpredictability. We all know about this from problems faced in attempting to predict future weather. There are so many variables involved, and the initial conditions from which the calculations begin are so difficult to define accurately, that even the largest computers in the world will never be able to do more than predict general trends. Nothing is guaranteed. The tip and tilt of some events is even more unpredictable than the tossing of a coin.

Expect the Unexpected

The progress of reality is a combination of order, resembling the workings of a predictable machine, and chaos, where unpredictability reigns. Statistics tell us that we can expect some things to happen – the sun will rise in the morning; a full moon will come when our diary says so; we will grow older each day. But chaos theory also tells us to expect the unexpected. We can never be sure of which of all possible futures will materialize. The future is not written in stone, it can work itself out in a multitude of ways. I love that definition of God from Simone Weil: 'He in whose wake the year unfolds

its days.' The world unfolds its days in different unpredictable ways, depending partly on all the small decisions we make.

This may seem all very far from our quiet meditative moment by the gatepost beneath the stars. But it is not. The future does not exist

The progress of reality is a combination of order, resembling the workings of a predictable machine, and chaos, where unpredictability reigns.

and cannot be totally known until it happens – because so many alternative, equally unpredictable paths are possible, only 'hardening' into reality when one of them materializes. This knowledge gives us some freedom in our lives, liberating us within certain bounds to determine our own destiny; move on in a new direction. We might change one of our habits, for instance; do something not done before; adopt a new attitude to some other person. We may, as we have grown older, have accepted 'limitations' to our behaviour and now realize that they have become false fences. A quiet moment's reflection can help us see that we don't have to be bound by past expectations, unquestioned habits, or the opinions of others.

CHAPTER SIX

THE PULL
OF GRAVITY

*It can be delightful to defy gravity. When the
wind is from the east, the sky over the South Downs
is full of paragliders drifting in slow circles above the
Sussex landscape; I see them from my garden, floating
up to the clouds like thistledown. We all, I suspect, have
a deep yearning to fly and often do so in dreams. But
most of the time we do not spare a second thought for
the force of gravity that holds us to the Earth.*

DEFYING GRAVITY

◆

The gentle force of gravity, to which we rarely give a second thought (despite the fact that as we grow older it quietly begins to dominate our lives), is remarkable in its creative power; it has not only shaped the stars, but without it, life could never have evolved.

THE DEEP PLEASURE AT DEFYING GRAVITY, if only for a brief moment, begins in childhood. I notice that with my grandchildren; they no sooner learn to walk than they want to jump – at first tentatively off the edge of a rug, tottering and turning to do it again; then off a shallow step, or more worryingly from the arm of a sofa into the cushions. Little Adam grins and applauds himself as he jumps from step to step down a path in the garden. This delight is not limited to our species: anyone who has paused to watch young lambs in the spring will have seen them leaping and gambolling together in small groups, with lamby gladness.

I have mentioned gravity several times now in connection with the practice of mindfulness. The object of the exercise is always to bring oneself back into the present moment. We begin to notice our bodies, letting go of the tension when we find muscles in the shoulders, back or legs too tight. We feel the pull of gravity as a soft pressure on our feet (and through the buttocks when we sit). It is quite a gentle force. I find that focusing on gravity's pull for a moment has an interesting

> **Notes to Grandchildren**
>
> • Take care of your own physical well-being, both when you are young and when you grow older. Go for a walk regularly – and swim, too. The practice of mindfulness will let you know what is good for you.

effect on my body; I instinctively straighten a little, not artificially, but gently opening up my shoulders, letting my lungs feel freer, gaining a better poise in my posture. I am here, now, and enjoying it.

As I get older, this physical awareness of poise becomes increasingly important. It is easy to give in to the pull of gravity, slowly letting the shoulders become rounder and more immobile over time; tempting, too, to avoid walking up hills, wondering if the climb and all the puffing are worth it. I don't have to think long, however, to know that it *is* worth it and I am fortunate in having the slopes of the South Downs to explore daily. Regular swimming is good, too; it opens up the lungs, gets the heart pumping and loosens the muscles.

The Unusual Nature of Gravity

Gravity is still something of a mystery to scientists, difficult to harmonize with the other forces of nature. Einstein tells us that it bends empty space, warping the universe around its galaxies and stars, planets, moons – and around the Earth. How can we possibly imagine that – that space can be bent? But however it functions, whatever the nature of this mysterious but familiar force, it plays a central role in our lives.

Like the air we breathe, often only noticed when it is polluted, gravity is taken for granted most of the time, ignored – until a favourite jug hits the floor and smashes. It is the invisible and gentle force that holds us down, grounding us where we are. Yet this is the force that created suns, pulling the clouds of interstellar gas and dust into spherical clumps, generating nuclear furnaces deep in their cores; it built the stars, that built the atoms, that built our bodies, that opened our minds to the here and now. Without gravity, none of the stars, nor the Earth, nor you and me would be here.

Despite that, gravity is a surprisingly weak force, *much* weaker than electricity or the power of a magnet. It may take its toll on the legs of those of us who are older when we toil our way up a hill; but it also takes the combined mass of the whole Earth to cause an autumn leaf to float gently to the ground, rocking this way and that, lifted for a moment by the breeze, then falling.

Contemplating Gravity

Aristotle, 'The Philosopher' referred to earlier, had some strange ideas about gravity. As we have already seen, he taught that heavy objects fall faster than light objects, a view that held sway until challenged by Galileo. It was not easy to test accurately Galileo's conviction that all objects fall at the same rate, because air resistance affects different objects in varying ways – a feather or a leaf float downwards buoyed up by the atmosphere; a lead weight plummets. But long after the principle was established as true, it was put to the test in an amusing experiment. Captain Dave Scott, commander of the 1971 Apollo space mission to Hadley Rill on the surface of the Moon (it was the first mission to use the Lunar Roving Vehicle), carried with him a feather. Taking advantage of the fact that the Moon has no atmosphere to interfere with the test, he performed an experiment on live TV, watched by millions. Holding the feather in one hand and a rock hammer in the other, he released them simultaneously. They hit the ground at the same time and Aristotle's dogma bit the dust once more!

Aristotle also taught that the reason objects fall to the ground is that the ground is their natural place and that is where they 'want' to be – not what we would call a scientific explanation. The world had to wait for the brilliant mathematician, Isaac Newton, for a more satisfactory explanation. His 'Law of Universal Gravitation' in 1687 was able to give a full account of falling objects.

Isaac Newton was born in 1642, the same year that Galileo died. Over three and a half centuries later he is still reckoned by many to be 'the greatest scientist that ever lived', vying for top position with Einstein. The sentiment of his epitaph by Alexander Pope has never really changed: *'Nature and nature's laws lay hid in night; / God said "Let Newton be" and all was light.'*

It was Newton's discovery that not only large masses like the Sun, Moon and Earth attract other objects (including each other), but that every particle in the universe must attract every other particle with a force of attraction that diminishes with distance. (Double the distance between two objects and the force is reduced to a quarter; treble the distance and it becomes a ninth of its strength – this is known as the inverse square law.)

THE MOON & GRAVITY

Since the Moon and the Earth attract each other, then it is natural to wonder when gazing up at the Moon why it does not fall to Earth and crush us all; yet it continues to sail serenely above the clouds without posing any threat.

LET US CONTEMPLATE THE MOON and let it be one of those lovely balmy nights late in August – the time of harvest in northern regions. The Sun has recently set and we may have time to watch the shadow of the Earth rising above the opposite horizon in the east, beneath the pinker dome of the sky; a broad mauve-grey curtain hinting at the coming night. In this growing band of shadow, a Harvest Moon appears, a bright golden sphere, creeping slowly up over the horizon from behind the silhouettes of distant trees. It looks enormous. But the increase in size, contrary to impression, is an illusion, caused by its image being in close proximity to the details of the distant landscape: it looks big in comparison. The first time I saw a harvest moon, it terrified me. I was about seven years old and out walking in a field not far from our house in Eskdale. Suddenly I noticed that the horizon appeared to be ablaze up on the fells and I thought a whole farm, with all the trees around it, must be on fire up on Birker Moor. I ran home to tell my father, but turning to look again as I climbed our garden fence I was astonished to see the Moon sailing free above the hill. It was a magical, heart-thumping moment. The Moon seemed ten times its normal size.

All an Illusion

Anyone who doubts that the size of a harvest moon is an illusion can perform a simple experiment: Hold your thumb at arm's length against the rising moon and note its size. Later that night, try again when it has swung high overhead and seems to be its 'normal' size once more. It may feel surprising but you will find the dimensions remain the same. Our minds can sometimes lead us astray.

The Magic of Momentum

Now that the Moon has risen free of the horizon, we can contemplate its mass: a ball of rock the size of Europe, 3,476 kilometres (2,160 miles) in diameter. And there it hangs serenely in the sky, coming no closer nor getting any bigger. Why does it not fall towards us as a cricket ball does when thrown into the sky? The answer comes from Newton's law of gravitation combined with Kepler's laws of planetary motion. The answer is that it *is* falling towards us, just as a cricket ball does as it descends, but it won't hit us because something else is happening. The Moon carries momentum from the time it was created, moving at a tangent to Earth, and so it is falling *around* us, rather than down onto us. That is what an orbit is.

In the Middle Ages, people had no idea of momentum or inertia: the only reason something moved, they believed, was that it was continuously being pushed. A cart stuck in mud on a country lane will stay where it is until shoulders are applied; it will stop as soon as the pushing stops. The reason that the Sun, Moon and planets continued to orbit the Earth (as they thought) was that they were pushed by angels.

'Momentum' has now become part of our vocabulary; football teams gather momentum in a World Cup when they move from winning game to winning game. This, of course, is an analogy, but it is based on an understanding of the Law of Inertia – the property of a body by which it resists any change in its velocity. It is inertia that causes a body to remain stationary in a state of rest (a teenager in bed – another analogy!), or to continue moving in a straight line unless diverted by a force such as gravity.

Lunar Momentum

The Moon has momentum, which carries it around the Earth rather than crashing apocalyptically down onto the surface. This momentum comes originally from the ring of rocks and debris that orbited the Earth in its early years, after a collision with another, smaller planet blasted the material into space. Similarly, the Earth and planets all orbit the Sun, rather than plunging into its fiery surface, because they have the momentum given to them by the rings of dust that orbited the Sun in its youth, and from which they were born, thanks to the force of gravity pulling all the material together into spheres.

Without gravity, our world would immediately fall apart, oceans lifting up into the sky, the atmosphere floating away, the molten interior of the Earth spilling out into space. The Sun would instantly explode, unable to contain the nuclear forces at its heart, the whole of our solar system quickly disappearing in darkness and chaos.

Standing by the Ocean

Now let us stand by the sea, this time to wait for a New Moon. It is a calm evening, waves rhythmically breaking on the beach, dragging at the shingle; a pair of small wading birds,

Turnstones, explore the rocks. It is sunset and the sky floods with colour, the red ball of the Sun sinking to the horizon, seeming enormous beyond a distant tiny boat. How would you describe this scene to an old friend who was born blind? It quickly becomes obvious that the words we use have severe limitations. Red? Ice blue? Silver sea? Big sky? We are forced to use analogies. How do we explain colour to someone who has never seen it? It is salutary to feel speechless for a moment, to contemplate this mystery that we can't always articulate what we want to convey.

But we are here to meditate on the Moon. The white crescent gets brighter as twilight leaves the sky. We may notice a small dark patch near the northern horn of the crescent, the first feature to appear to the unaided eye; it is a great plain over 320 kilometres (200 miles) in diameter, named *Mare Crisium* or the Sea of Crises. And then we may notice the dark side of the moon, the 'old moon in the new moon's arms'. The Sun has not yet risen on this part of the lunar surface, but it is not in total darkness because the lunar landscape is bathed in light reflected from the Earth – 'earthlight', like moonlight but much brighter. No one has ever stood on the dark side of the moon to observe the earth shadows and compare them to moon shadows back here on Earth.

A dozen astronauts have stood in the blazing sunshine that spreads across the surface after new moon, and they have looked up at the Earth. We might have imagined that anyone on the Moon would look *down* on the Earth, not up to it. Then we remember that down and up are just relative words – whichever way gravity pulls us is down; and on the Moon the weaker lunar gravity pulls an astronaut (who will there weigh only a dozen kilos) down onto the lunar ground and from there he or she looks *up* at the Earth, itself hanging in the sky like a giant moon.

Dave Scott, who performed Galileo's experiment with a feather and a rock hammer, told me once that the Earth is very beautiful and fragile seen from the Moon; it looks like a glorious Christmas-tree decoration, blue, green and white. 'But you know, Adam – there was a philosophical side to that lunar mission that we were not prepared for, it was not part of our training with NASA.' There was clearly something he would have liked to have said about seeing Mother Earth hanging in space – it had struck him forcibly; but he did not have the means to explore it with words, rather like the mystery we would face when trying to describe all the colours of a sunset to a blind person.

Tidal Ebb & Flow

We have been watching the Moon now for a little time and it is slowly following the Sun, to set soon beyond the dark line of the ocean. We may have noticed that the waves are now breaking on the beach further away from us, as the tide ebbs. It is the gravity of the Moon pulling on the waters of the

> ### Gardening by the Moon
>
> Many gardeners believe that the Moon still has its influence on life and growth. I have always planted my potatoes on Good Friday, without really considering why; it was a tradition I picked up in childhood. It was only recently, when reading an article about gardening by the phases of the Moon, that I discovered the origin of the practice; it is close to the time of Full Moon, the best time apparently for planting root crops, when it was believed by those gardeners that the moisture was rising.

Earth, changing the sea level where we stand, perhaps by a metre in the time we have been loitering. Some evolutionary biologists take the view that it was the regular tidal ebb and flow of water in shallow lagoons long ago that created ideal conditions for life to evolve on Earth. Without this tidal movement, our distant ancestors would not have evolved and consequently we would not be here to contemplate the lovely phenomenon. We owe our lives to the Moon.

Galileo got the tides wrong. Since Newton was born in the year that he died, Galileo did not have the benefit of knowing about the Law of Universal Gravitation. Galileo's big task was to convince his contemporaries that the Earth was moving, turning on its axis and orbiting the Sun. The problem for him was that, although it made sense mathematically and also from what he had observed through his telescope, he couldn't actually prove it. He thought that the tides had come to his rescue, suggesting that the reason they regularly slopped up and down our beaches, like milk carried in a pail, was because of the Earth's daily movement. Now we know otherwise: that the gravitational pull of the Moon (and to a lesser extent the Sun) causes the tide to rise and fall.

Daily, the Moon moves billions of tons of water effortlessly; why do we not make better use of this display of energy? There is a small, comparatively unsung museum that I know out on the salt marshes at Ayamonte in southern Spain. It used to be a tide mill, catching the sea water at high tide in a man-made lagoon, and then releasing it through mill races to drive four great stone wheels that ground the corn. What a marvellous use of free energy! An instructive notice on the museum wall claims that in the eighteenth century there were as many as a thousand such tide mills around the coasts of Europe, all of them drawing their energy ultimately from the gravity of the moon. I am astonished that we have not made more of this simple technology. As we adapt to living in a world with an increasing population, while learning to cope with global warming, it would surely be a good thing to give up our dependence on fossil fuels, and turn our attention to energy sources that are both clean and virtually limitless.

CHAPTER SEVEN

ARE WE ALONE IN THE UNIVERSE?

*We shall never be able to prove that we are
the only conscious species in the universe; but one
whisper of an intelligent communication from space
will prove the contrary once and for all. The search for
extraterrestrial intelligence (SETI), using radio
telescopes and computers, is one of the most exciting
projects recently taken up by science. A positive
discovery will alter the way we think
about ourselves for ever.*

THE CANALS OF MARS

◆

It has become a feature of folk culture to imagine visitors from space as Martians, aliens from our close neighbour in the solar system, the Red Planet. H.G. Wells exploited this idea in his famous novel of 1897, The War of the Worlds, in which the invaders are more threatening than mere 'little green men'.

A BOOK THAT HAS EXCITED MY THINKING since I was in my teens sits on the bottom shelf in my study among the larger volumes: Hutchinson's *Splendour of the Heavens, Vol. 1*, published in 1923. It has green board covers with a leather spine, the lettering in gold. When I had my first telescope, it was a book I took out from the local library so many times I almost felt I owned it. Then we moved as a family to Somerset, via Canada, and I lost touch with the cherished volume, until many years later when I secured a second-hand copy through the internet.

It was the coloured plates showing the stars seen from Westminster Bridge each month that first caught my imagination; they were my first guide to the constellations. The London skyline included silhouettes of the House of Commons looking south, and St Paul's Cathedral looking north against a pink sunset glow; above the pink, the dome of the sky was midnight blue dotted with stars joined by thin dashed lines to delineate each constellation. I had never been to

London in those days and I found these star charts unbeliev-
ably romantic. The heavens were opening up to me.

Dreaming of Other Worlds

It was another plate in the book that intrigued me for a different reason and aroused the question 'Are we alone?'. Are
there other worlds, where people have built buildings like St
Paul's Cathedral? In a chapter on Mars there is a fanciful
depiction of the surface of the Red Planet; a pink sandstorm
obliterates the horizon beneath a dark sky, while the landscape is criss-crossed by a geometric network of lines – the
canals of Mars. What excitement it was to contemplate that
illustration. An Italian observer, Schiaparelli, had first
observed linear features on the planet's surface in 1877 and
speculated that it was a dying world, subject to increasing
drought. The inhabitants, a civilization approaching extinction, had created the network of canals to carry water from
polar ice caps to irrigate their parched land, creating the sort
of narrow belts of agriculture we find along the banks of the
River Nile. To be caught up in that idea was thrilling and I
remember imagining pyramids and sphinxes being enveloped
in sand as the Martian deserts slowly choked the whole planet
– and wondering what the Martians looked like.

Later observers put together elaborate maps of the canal
system: I have one here in front of me as I write, in a 1910
book called *Mars as the Abode of Life* by Percival Lowell of Flagstaff

Observatory in Arizona. It seemed that now we had proof that intelligent life existed beyond the Earth. No doubt it was the convictions of people like Lowell that fuelled a growing interest in the twentieth century in UFOs (Unidentified Flying Objects), flying saucers, flashing lights and tabloid tales about visitors from space.

We were not the first to dream of other worlds like this. Greek philosophers speculated about their possible existence; Norse, Hindu and Buddhist mythology almost took them for granted. The great English astronomer William Herschel, who in 1781 discovered the planet Uranus, wondered if the lunar craters were circular cities, while Kepler, Galileo's contemporary and discoverer of the Laws of Planetary Motion, wrote a fantasy story about giant serpents inhabiting the Moon, shedding their sun-baked skins nightly. Imagination was driven by hope.

In 1958 I built a large Newtonian telescope in the garden (it had its own observatory), mostly for making maps of selected areas of the Moon. One night I spent hours peering at Mars as it passed high overhead and in odd moments of clear 'seeing' spotted some of the major canals – brief glimpses of web-like patterns on the surface of the planet. I had longed to see these signs of alien life and it was a deeply satisfying experience.

The trouble is – the canals don't exist. A few years later, in 1964, the space probe *Mariner 4* sent back the first photographs of the Martian surface and the canals had vanished. They were an illusion created and built up in the mind; expectation and desire had joined up the dots and marks on the surface and made them into a complex map. It is salutary to discover how easily our minds can be mislead when we want to be and are not careful.

Venus, the Greenhouse World

Our dreaming of life on other worlds did not end with Mars; Venus was another possibility, at least for vegetable life. The Evening or Morning Star, always close to sunset or sunrise because of its inner orbit in the solar system, has caught the attention of anyone who has the briefest acquaintance with the night sky; nothing, apart from the Moon, is brighter. Galileo was the first to observe, with his telescope, the planet's changing crescent shape, proving that it was in orbit around the Sun and not around the Earth. This sister planet is the size of our own world; Earth would look much the same seen from Venus, perhaps a little bluer. But Venus is always completely shrouded in cloud, allowing us, until recently, to dream of alien jungles and exotic flowers; maybe it even supported some dinosaur-like creatures. There *could* be life – a rich alternative ecosystem – no one could tell us otherwise: that is, until the Soviet probe Venera 7 landed on the planet in 1970. We now know it to be a totally inhospitable world, a planet suffocating from a dense atmosphere of carbon dioxide, the result of a runaway 'greenhouse effect' (Earth beware!), with acid rain, planet-wide thunderstorms and gigantic bolts of lightning; in other words, a veritable hell.

The Goldilocks Planet

It seems that our own planet is the only one to support life in the solar system. We are in what has been dubbed 'the Goldilocks position', orbiting the sun in the zone where it is neither too hot nor too cold, but just right, where water can exist in its liquid form. There may be bacteria in the soil of Mars and simple-celled organisms may inhabit Titan, the methane-shrouded moon of Saturn; something primitive may even lurk in the ocean beneath the all-embracing icecap of Europa, the giant moon of Jupiter. So far we have no evidence of any of this. But as for intelligent life able to ask philosophical questions such as 'Who am I?', we are certainly the only ones in the immediate galactic neighbourhood.

We have to turn elsewhere in our search for other intelligent beings. Opinion as to whether we will be successful or not is divided and hinges on a major question: is the evolution of life a natural consequence of chemistry in a world built from the elements in the periodic table – and therefore bound to arise eventually, as sure as weeds grow on empty ground? Or was the emergence of complex molecules leading to the building of DNA, those molecular threads of information in the cells of all living beings, an isolated and unrepeatable accident, unique to Planet Earth? Is life a natural self-assembling phenomenon as I believe or a freak occurrence in an otherwise dead universe?

I take the view that the physics and chemistry of this universe inevitably lead to biology, and that the process of evolution then takes over, causing increasingly complex life forms to emerge. Some astronomers have gone so far as to suggest that this galaxy alone may house upwards of ten thousand intelligent civilizations (a calculation based upon a number of conservative guesstimates, such as how many Sun-like stars there are, how many Earth-like planets, on what percentage of these will life have taken hold etc). Already the astronomical community is making great advances in discovering planets, called exo-planets, orbiting other suns; most of them are vast, the size of Jupiter or bigger. But some are small and potentially Earth-like and inhabiting 'Goldilocks' zones.

I take the view that the physics and chemistry of this universe inevitably lead to biology.

One day we might wake to exciting headlines 'Alien Intelligence detected in the constellation of Orion' – or some such. I hope it will be in my lifetime, but that becomes increasingly unlikely. Perhaps my grandchildren will hear the great news, and I wonder how the world will take it. And what form will the alien intelligence take – will it be anything like us? Will it be more gracious?

WHY ARE WE LIKE WE ARE?

◆

To probe the question about whether or not there are other intelli-
gent civilizations among the stars, we need to approach it from a
different angle and ask what we ourselves are doing in our corner of
this vast and ancient universe.

WE RETURN TO THE QUESTION we considered earlier:
'Who am I?' We found then that one answer has to
involve the knowledge that we are built from star dust. But
now let's try again.

Tonight I have chosen to follow Antares (meaning the 'Rival
of Mars'), a red giant star in the constellation of Scorpio, far
to the south; I could have selected any star but I have become
particularly fond of Antares. It is one of the brighter stars in
the sky and always near the horizon on summer nights when
seen from where I live, and so offers me the luxury of not
having to crane my neck, which I find less flexible these days.
Antares burns dull red, like a live coal, just above the dark
line of a hedge or through the lower branches of a tree.
Briefly, I remind myself of what we know about this star –
a massive sun over three hundred times the diameter of our
own Sun and shining from the period of history when Oliver
Cromwell was marching through England fighting for a
commonwealth and destroying religious images. Long ago,
it was worshipped in China as a protection against fire and

also credited with having great influence on the rearing of silk worms. I know that it is creating at its heart the atoms that build creatures like me.

And I ask again that difficult question: 'Who am I?' I know who I am, but when I look around within my feelings, do a scan of my body and the thoughts of my mind, there is nothing specific I can identify as 'me'. If I am honest, I find nothing there when I look for 'me', just the experience of being conscious, observing my body, feeling the night air on my skin. It could be described as an 'emptiness' or as a 'void' at the heart of my awareness. The Buddha used this sort of language when speaking of the reality that he believed lies behind all superficial phenomena, naming it *sunyata,* emptiness. But his emptiness is not your usual emptiness: to discover it is described as a 'great awakening'.

The Mystery of Consciousness

I find something strangely comforting – and not at all troubling – about this experience of consciousness that cannot be pinned down. *Consciousness* is a mystery that has emerged on Earth through the multi-million year evolution of our nervous systems. It exists in varying degrees throughout the animal kingdom. We might call it 'mind' or 'spirit' or 'soul'.

It is in identifying myself as a conscious being that I begin to have a deeper answer to the question 'Who am I?'. It has taken untold ages for the self-assembling chemistry of life to

'It is the most basic religious belief that consciousness and value are at the heart of reality.' produce beings like you and me who are able to ask these questions as we stand looking at the stars. In us, the universe, after 13.7 billion years, has woken up to the delight of awareness. With this thought, I find myself recollecting the Hindu myth about Brahman the soul of the universe, who in a unitary state of conscious bliss, named *Sat-Chit-Ananda,* decided in an act of playfulness to hide himself in his opposite, the multiple world of dark sleeping matter. Through aeons of reincarnation through rocks, plants, animals and people, he is rediscovering his original self – mindful meditation opening doors to this world soul.

Each culture has found different ways to speak about the emergence of consciousness on Earth. A contemporary theologian I admire, Professor Keith Ward, has written: 'It is the most basic religious belief that consciousness and value are at the heart of reality.' The intuition here is that the existence of the universe is itself evidence of Creative Intelligence. That creative intelligence we may like to identify with God, or with an 'Unknown Something'. Another theologian, one with the training of a scientist, has commented that the universe 'seems shot through with mind'. If these thoughts be true, then in allowing ourselves to become aware of our consciousness in our practice of mindfulness, we are opening ourselves to the intelligence that creates the cosmos. This would be how I understand the biblical language that says we are made in the image of God. Though still in our infancy as a species, and flawed spiritual creatures, we could think of ourselves as incarnations of the mind that lies behind all things.

Work in Progress

My own conclusion is that consciousness has emerged and is emerging throughout the universe and not just here on Earth. It will only be a matter of time before we make contact with another civilization – a much more dramatic moment for future history than Columbus's discovery of the New World and its people, or a European's first encounter with the aborigines of Australia. People evolved on another world may be very unlike us physically, but our consciousness will be the same, raising the same questions and the same problems, discovering the same laws of physics and assembling the same periodic table of elements. Communication, however, will be challenging, not because of language difficulties (code-breakers will be able to handle that rapidly) but because of the distances involved. A message travelling at the top speed of light from a world in our own close neighbourhood of the Milky Way Galaxy could take perhaps three hundred years to arrive; an answer from us would reach them three hundred years later – little more than waving the message: 'We are here!'

Our Moral Compass

Where do we find the moral guidance for living our lives? How do we know how to behave, how to relate to other people? It is in recognizing that consciousness has emerged in us, through a long process of evolution within the material of the universe, that I believe we may find our moral compass. We each of us from earliest childhood build up a picture of the world around us, discovering how to relate to the people that fill it. We still have the option, of course, as conscious creative beings with free will, to put 'self' first and to live selfish self-seeking lives. We will then treat other people as disposable characters passing through our world. It is easy, almost natural, to let ourselves be dragged that way.

A more fulfilling view is to accept that other people and other living beings are each at the centre of their *own* worlds. We will then find ourselves relating to them with respect (even though sometimes this may be very difficult), acknowledging that they should be treated just as we would like to be treated. From this realization flow all the best ethical systems that have emerged with human culture, such as the Ten Commandments. One of the most rewarding things about life, I find as I grow older, is in being able to feel glad and grateful about being part of the creative living process.

WHAT THE STARS FORETELL

The popularity of star signs and horoscopes in newspapers and magazines suggests that readers still entertain an interest in astrology, believing that there is a link between the heavens and what happens in their daily lives on Earth.

THE MORE WE CONTEMPLATE THE UNIVERSE, the more personal it becomes. We begin to suspect that the self-assembling laws of nature are guaranteed over time to produce people (of whatever shape or form) and that conscious mind was there, dormant, in the early universe, waiting to emerge. Perhaps this sense that mind or spirit is an essential and inevitable part of the universe provides us with an explanation for the popularity of astrology. It is the feeling that we are connected to everything else, though in ways we may not have understood, that suggests a link with the stars.

It may come as a surprise to some that Galileo, 'Father of Modern Science', cast horoscopes. He was familiar with astrology from when he taught astronomy to medical students – in those days, doctors needed to be able to cast horoscopes to see what the stars foretold of patients' lives, as an aid to their treatment. We know that Galileo himself prepared many horoscopes, including one for his daughter Virginia (later the nun Marie Celeste) at her birth and another for the ailing Grand Duke Ferdinand. It is suspected, however, that he had little faith in these forecasts, believing that such prophecies were only ever found to be true with hindsight, *after* their fulfilment.

It was the long shadow of Aristotle, who linked the various organs of the body to the planets and zodiacal signs, that kept the door open to the idea that the lives of men were written in the stars. Galileo's contemporary, Kepler, was still able to assume the truths of astrology as a matter of course. He despised the superstition and quackery of popular prophecies, but suspected that deep down there was something in astrology to be respected, writing that 'nothing exists nor happens in the visible sky that is not sensed in some hidden manner by the faculties of Earth and Nature'.

Astrology & The Night Sky

We may share with Galileo doubts about the relevance of the position of Sun, Moon and planets at our birth, their movements through the various signs of the zodiac; but astrology does have to deal with some of the most interesting regions of the night sky. My favourite spread of constellations is visible in winter in northern latitudes when there is frost on the ground and your breath is visible on the night air. Aries, Taurus, Gemini and Cancer arc across the sky, and, as the night progresses, Leo follows on: a ram, a bull, twin boys, a crab and a lion. Our inherited mythology has made the heavens come alive, made them personal. It is in these constellations of the zodiac that we are most likely to notice the Moon and the wandering planets, where you can follow their slow movements, month by month.

Taurus

Let us begin with Taurus, which in December is high up in the sky to the south on a December evening. Here is a constellation that looks like what it purports to be, a cluster of stars in the shape of a bull's head with horns lowered for charging, its

---

The Precession of the Equinoxes

There is a slow movement in the heavens that a lifetime of naked-eye observing would not detect. It affects the twelve signs of the zodiac, causing them to drift out of position; Aries through Pisces to Aquarius (dubbing our era the Age of Aquarius), Taurus back through Aries to Pisces and so forth. This phenomenon, known as the 'Precession of the Equinoxes', is due to a slow wobble in the Earth's axis as it spins. It takes about 24,000 years for one gyration of the axis, slowly shifting the coordinates of the sky as it does so. Roughly every two thousand years, one sign of the zodiac slips across into the neighbouring constellation. Somehow this does not seem to have confused modern-day astrologers!

bright eye being the first magnitude star Aldebaran. As I look at Aldebaran, I see it as it was when I was a boy of nine, just starting to be fascinated by the night sky; it is sixty-five light years distant. The stars around it, forming the bull's head, are in fact not close to it at all – they form a cluster called the Hyades and are 150 light years away, far beyond Aldebaran. That whole cluster is drifting at something like 20 kilometres (12.5 miles) per second towards Betelgeuse in Orion, movement an observer would not notice in a whole lifetime.

Hovering over the back of the bull like a swarm of fireflies is another famous cluster, the Pleiades, sometimes called the Seven Sisters, mentioned over two thousand years ago in the biblical Book of Job. Anyone with good eyesight may be able to count ten stars in the cluster, but the whole group seen through a telescope, is rich in fainter stars; photographs reveal wisps of interstellar cloud, indicating that the whole cluster is young, its stars being only fifty million years old.

Gemini

Swing the eyes left of Taurus and we come to Gemini, its two brightest stars being Castor and Pollux, the twins of Greek mythology. It is Castor, the more northerly of the pair, that intrigues me most. Viewed through a telescope, it turns out to be a triple system of suns, orbiting their common centre of gravity. Two are blue giants, while the third is a small red dwarf. At greater magnification, each of the three reveals itself to be a double star: Castor is a complex system of six suns. If there is also a world there that can support life then what an extraordinary place it must be, with four blue suns and two red ones; sunsets must be particularly dramatic!

South of, and below, Gemini is Orion the Hunter with its bright star Betelgeuse, a stellar red giant already mentioned earlier. Orion is another of the few constellations that vaguely look like what their names imply – a giant straddling the sky, with head, shoulders, feet, belt and dagger. The brilliant Sirius, the Dog Star, follows the hunter across the heavens. The rising of Sirius in the early morning, incidentally, marked the date in Ancient Egypt of the annual flooding of the Nile; this information, passed to him from his astronomers, gave the Pharaoh great power because it meant he was able to predict the rising waters that were so essential to farming. He could even pretend to command the Nile to flood.

In contemplating this part of the sky, it is perhaps the dagger hanging from Orion's three-starred belt that offers the most interest. Imbedded in the belt is a faint patch of nebulosity. Closer inspection, even with binoculars, reveals a star nursery – a clutch of new hot suns, already born, illuminate the clouds of interstellar gas that surround them. Long-exposure photographs are stunning in their beautiful detail. Because of the distance and time lag, we actually see them as they were in the days when the Roman Empire had just come to an end, 1,500 years ago. Perhaps one day new worlds will be formed and life will evolve on planets in that nebula – but we cannot peer too far into the future, because here we speculate about events billions of years down the line.

Cancer & Leo

As the night progresses, our eyes pass over the constellation of Cancer; there are no bright stars here but we may pause for a moment to catch a glimpse of a faint star cluster known as the Beehive. Formerly this small cluster was called Praesepe, meaning 'the manger', and stars to each side were named 'the donkeys'.

The following sign of the zodiac is Leo. A seventeenth-century manuscript, written not long after the death of Galileo, says of anyone born under this sign that they 'are very faithful, keeping their promises with all punctuality … prudent and of incomparable judgement…', which must be very encouraging for those whose birthdays lie between July 24 and August 23, when the Sun is said to inhabit the sign. The brightest star in the constellation, Regulus, lies almost exactly on the path the Moon takes as it orbits the Earth. Sometimes the Moon passes in front of Regulus and the event is well worth watching.

Each night the Moon swings across the sky from east to west with all the stars as the world turns daily on its axis. At the same time, the Moon is slowly moving towards the east against the background of stars as it pursues its monthly orbit. If you were to notice by chance one night that Regulus lay just

a little to the left of the Moon (as seen from northern countries), then wait and watch. Very slowly the limb of the Moon moves towards the star, until with a hesitant flicker the star fades and vanishes behind a lunar mountain range, as that massive ball of rock continues its momentous journey.

Notes to Grandchildren

• Make yourself familiar with the night sky: the knowledge will be a great investment. Apart from any other pleasure it may bring, it will help you know where to look in the sky if we discover that we are not alone in the universe.

• Practise kindness in all your relationships.

• The golden rule – always to treat others in the way you would like them to treat you (found in one form or another in all spiritual traditions) – is not just about how you relate to other people in your world. You have to recognize that each of them is the centre of their own world. Respect their world.

• Sex is a powerful driving force that has got us here through millions of years of evolution. Show it respect. Be mindful in all your relationships and always seek to build up the other person's self-esteem.

• Respect and acknowledge those people whom others do not notice.

CHAPTER EIGHT

WISDOM, DISASTERS & DEEP TIME

Traditional superstition has it that our lives
can be 'ill-starred', that disasters are caused by our
links to the cosmos: the very word 'disaster' is formed
from the Latin for star — astrum — with the prefix 'dis'
implying something torn asunder. Illness too was
believed to have its roots in the heavens; 'influenza' is
from the Italian, referring directly to the influence of
the stars. Wisdom grasps the truth that along with
order, there is sometimes disorder, chaos. It is beneficial
to remember that it was an asteroid colliding with
Earth that wiped out the dinosaurs.

METEORS & SHOOTING STARS

◆

For thousands of years, people have looked to the heavens for guidance, wondering at the appearance of those transient visitors from space, shooting stars (a symbol in Buddhism of the ephemeral nature of life), marvelling at, and sometimes worshipping, the rare rocks that fall from the sky.

SITTING ON MY DESK I HAVE SOME SMALL CHUNKS of iron-stone that fell from the sky; they are bits of meteorite I once picked up in the desert in the USA. It is intriguing to hold them, knowing that they have had a mysterious billion-year history orbiting the Sun in the deep cold of space before colliding with Earth fifty thousand years ago. Recently our news channels were full of video footage of a large lump of rock that tore through the skies over Russia in 2013, shattering windows with its thunder, exploding with mega-tonne power. An even more massive meteorite, perhaps the ice core of a comet, exploded above Siberia in 1908, flattening thousands of hectares of forest. The universe can be a dangerous and destructive place.

Not only is the universe dangerous but, in detail, it is unpredictable. Perhaps this accounts for our fascination with shooting stars – or at least *my* fascination. Their unexpected appearance is always thrilling, making me catch my breath. 'Make a wish!' say some people, with the belief that the future has the ability to surprise us with unanticipated blessings — which it does. Some of the best things in my life have happened without my planning them.

The Perseids

A favourite night of the year is the 12th of August, when Earth in its orbit passes through the trail left by an old comet called Swift-Tuttle. Tiny pieces of dust and grit collide with our atmosphere at the prodigious speed of 60 kilometres (37 miles) per second, and burn up so fast that a companion observer has no time to turn their head. 'Oh! Wow!' — 'Where?' goes the breathless conversation. These are the Perseid meteors, named as such because they seem to fall down the sky from the northern constellation of Perseus; they are also known as 'The Tears of St Lawrence'.

I try to catch sight of a few Perseids every August (they go on falling for a few days after the 12th) and have done so for well over sixty years. One of the best years was soon after I first met my wife, Ros; we took a bottle of wine and a blanket up to a high point on the Downs, with a good command of the

A favourite night of the year is the 12th of August, when Earth in its orbit passes through the trail left by an old comet called Swift-Tuttle.

whole sky. You never know where the next meteor is going to be, the anticipation being part of the fun and the thrill; we tried to keep count but gave up after seventy.

Order & Chaos

It would be simplistic to believe that contemplating the night sky is always going to inspire calm and comfortable thoughts of happy security. The world, the universe, even our lives exhibit order and predictability, but lurking beneath the surface there is also disorder and creative chaos. Wisdom recognizes that both have their place. There are many things we do not know and cannot anticipate – and cannot, by the very nature of things, ever predict.

The world has been jolted by the unpredictable many times, the last major event being the impact and explosion of a comet or asteroid 63 million years ago, which so devastated the planet that it brought to an end the era of dinosaurs, creatures that successfully ruled the Earth for 135 million years. The giant 180-kilometre (112-mile) diameter Chicxulub crater caused by that event is now almost lost beneath the geology of the Yucatan peninsula in Central America. A pair of binoculars, however, will show the sun rising or setting on similar-sized craters on the Moon, where they have been preserved from change since being formed in a period of catastrophic bombardment earlier in the formative history of the solar system.

'Nothing to do with us', we may be tempted to feel about events of so long ago. We would be wrong. Without that traumatic shake-up of the ecosystem we probably would not be here; the extinction of so many species, including the dinosaurs, cleared the ground for the evolution of our remote ancestors, tiny shrew-like creatures, as mammals came to dominate the Earth. Out of chaos comes life from elephants and whales to mice and men. Wisdom dictates that both order and disorder have their part to play.

Comets – Fingers of Doom?

It is perhaps due to a deeper recognition of the creative role of the unexpected that led people not only to make wishes on shooting stars, but also to feel disturbed by the appearance of comets. Despite their ethereal beauty, comets have traditionally been seen as harbingers of doom; in Galileo's day, three comets that all appeared in the autumn skies of 1618 were interpreted by many (with hindsight) to be heralds of the Thirty Years' War.

Galileo himself missed them – he was ill throughout that autumn, his only interest in comets being in their nature, which he got wrong. The majority of people still believed, as they had since Aristotle, that comets were an atmospheric phenomenon, coming and going in the imperfect sublunary regions. Galileo, perhaps surprisingly, tended to agree; being fuzzy objects ('hairy stars'), their size and actual distance from Earth was hard to measure, so he was content to fall back for once on received thinking.

We now know that a typical comet is a mountain-sized conglomeration of rock and ice, a 'dirty snowball' that falls into the central parts of the solar system from deep space on an eccentric orbit, only growing its tail, its 'finger of doom', as the Sun melts some of the ice and then wafts the vapour mist away with the solar wind. It is commonly held that it was comets that brought their ice crashing to Earth, so turning us into a watery planet. Without them, life would not have evolved to where it is today. It can be an entertaining thought, when taking a gin and tonic outside on a balmy summer evening, that the original source of the ice in the glass was the ice of a comet, frozen for most of its billions of years of history in deep space at temperatures approaching ultimate zero.

A typical comet is a mountain-sized conglomeration of rock and ice.

The Future of Planet Earth

One last thought about disasters that hit the world. Future historians, if there are such people, and if they write about us, and look deep beneath the surface of events, will judge our era according to the way we have handled our relationships. Not just those relationships within marriage or among family members, but relationships between religions and between

Letting Go of Certainties

Part of the joy of growing older, I find, is in letting go of certainties and living without answers. We don't know what comes next, any more than we can predict or command the appearance of a shooting star. We don't know, for example, (until perhaps the very end) when we are going to die, or how. I think that when one is young, it is natural to fear death – to be quietly horrified at the thought of non-existence. And yet, to state the obvious, it comes to all of us.

Personally, I have let go of all dreams of life in paradise after death, or of reincarnation, and prefer to live in the present. I was born in 1940 and so wasn't around anywhere in any sense in, say, 1935. Does that disturb me? No, not at all. Why should it? By the same token, why should it concern me that I will not be around in the years after I die? I am happy to go to rest with the thought on death from Ecclesiastes Chapter 12: '… when the dust returns to the earth from which it came, and the spirit returns to God who gave it.'

Galileo, who with his telescope began the process of revealing the true nature of the universe and our place in it, died in 1642 after debilitating illness. He almost certainly believed that he would go to Heaven, no doubt carried on the prayers of his daughter Sister Maria Celeste. Perhaps he did.

sects within religions; between nation states; between races. But most of all, perhaps, they will judge us on the way we have related to the rest of the natural world.

Never, in the whole of human history, has mankind's stewardship of the planet been more important than it is today. We are overrunning the landscapes and seascapes of the world and in danger of ruining them. We may be responsible for the largest swathe of extinctions in the planet's history, worse in the long run than the disaster that hit the dinosaurs. It is essential that we wake up to the fact that our links with the kingdoms of insects, birds, fish and animals, the worlds of plants, trees and bacteria, are intimate and inextricable. We depend upon each other, all part of one rising tide of evolving life. This is the wisdom we have uncovered in our contemplations of the night skies and our evolving place in the universe. The rich ecosystem on Earth, of which we are an emerging part, is a complex web of interconnections and mutual dependencies. We have to learn to love it.

Notes to Grandchildren

• Respect and love Nature.

• Support anyone who shows practical care for our ecosystem, whether for butterflies, birds, forests, seas…

DEEP TIME

◆

*As we grow older, time seems to fly by with increasing speed; and yet
there are moments when time hangs still, moments to cherish, giving
us time to watch the twilight leave the sky; time to listen to the rain.*

A N ASPECT OF THE UNIVERSE UNCOVERED since the days
of Galileo is its immense age and the brevity of all
human life on this planet. It was geological evidence from the
rocks that first revealed deep time. Paradoxically, it is through
awareness of the immense ages that preceded our appearance
on Earth that we can come to value the present moment.

Among the clutter on my desk, by the jug of pencils and
paintbrushes, the coloured inks and postcards, the accumulation of years of picking up rocks and fossils, and near to the
pot containing bits of shooting star, there is a heavy lump of
stone from the Yorkshire moors. I found it in the bed of a
stream when walking over the Pennines near Hebden Bridge,
where I was vicar at the time. It looks like a segment of a
snake with a central spine and a regular pattern of small hol-
lows. In actual fact, it is a 300-million-year-old chunk of
fossilized root of a tropical tree fern from the Carboniferous
era, when the world's coal seams were laid down. Yorkshire
was a hotter place in those days, and nearer the equator.

When I look out of my study window I can see the corner
of garden where I grow only ferns, with their wonderful

unfurling fiddleheads, and those strange spindly plants called horsetails. These are the descendents of vegetation that covered the Earth long before the evolution of flowering plants and, with the fossil on my desk, remind me how recently human beings appeared in the ecosystem.

We considered earlier how hard it is to comprehend the vast scale of the universe, the distances of even the closest stars. Gazing out into space puts an exhilarating strain on the imagination. We also discovered then that when looking up at the sky we are always peering back in time. But how very *much* time only slowly began to dawn on astronomers as they probed the vast, unbounded deep first revealed by Galileo and his telescope.

The Truth of Evolution

Thinking about the age of the universe was hampered in the West by a literal reading of the biblical creation stories in Genesis. The world in that theology was a small stage and its story began less than six thousand years ago. Many fundamentalist Christians, particularly in America, unfortunately still cling to this timescale. Buddhist thinking was never inhibited in this way; the world was ancient according to its philosophers, time measured in aeons. And an aeon, we are led to understand, is the time it would take to rub away a great mountain by stroking it with a silk cloth once every hundred years. Buddhists were well prepared for deep time!

It was in the study of the rocks of the Earth that a timescale matching the enormous dimensions of space, revealed by astronomy, became apparent. Geologists discovered the immense eras involved in the building and erosion of mountains; alternating layers of sandstone, shale and limestone revealed the remains of ancestral seas. Earth's autobiography, recorded in the rocks, spans four billion years.

There have been many attempts to convey in simple terms the age of the universe. My favourite is the one that compares the whole of time since the Big Bang, 13.7 billion years ago, as a shelf of books. Fourteen volumes of an encyclopaedia, each volume containing five hundred pages, represent the age of the universe. Life only emerges from the sea halfway through the final volume. The final quarter of the last line in the book covers all of human history since the end of the last Ice Age, ten thousand years ago. The whole of the twentieth century fits into the final full stop.

When I stand beneath the open sky at night I find the years fall away; my age becomes irrelevant. I am brought back home to the present moment. We human beings are so very, *very*, new. And it took a vast and ancient universe to give birth to the living environment from which we and all other creatures emerged, and are still emerging. Creation is a continuous process and we all of us, plants, insects, fish, birds, animals, human beings, sustain one another in this rich biosphere that coats the planet. I think that makes us all rather special.

ENDNOTES

1. *Galileo's Daughter: A Drama of Science, Faith and Love*, Dava Sobel (Harper Collins: Fourth Estate, London, 1999)
2. *What the Buddha Taught*, Walpola Rahula (Gordon Fraser, Bedford, UK, 1959)
3. *The Periodic Table*, Primo Levi (Abacus Books, London, 1986)
4. *Four Generations Project*. www.gallmannkenya.org/fourgenerations.html

BIBLIOGRAPHY

Ammonites & Leaping Fish, Penelope Lively (Fig Tree: Penguin Books, London, 2013)
Astronomy: A Brief History, Adam Ford (EBook in HistoryWorld's Pocket History Series, 2012)
A Short History of Nearly Everything, Bill Bryson (Transworld, London, 2003)
Feral: Rewilding the Land, Sea and Human Life, George Monbiot (Penguin Books, London, 2014)
Galileo, John L. Heilbron (Oxford University Press, Oxford, UK, 2010)
Late Youth: An Anthology Celebrating the Joys of Being Over Fifty, Susanna Johnston (Arcadia Books Ltd, London, 2005)
Somewhere Towards the End, Diana Athill (Granta Books, London, 2009)
The Rocks Don't Lie: A Geologist Investigates Noah's Flood, David. R. Montgomery (W.W. Norton & Company, New York, 2012)
The Stars in Our Heaven: Myths and Fables, Peter Lum (Thames and Hudson, London, 1932)

ACKNOWLEDGEMENTS

Thanks to Monica Perdoni, commissioning editor, for her support; Jenni Davis, my editor, for pruning and adjusting my text with an easy wisdom; and of course the design team, Peter Bridgewater and Ginny Zeal.

INDEX

Aldebaran 126
Altair 53, 61, 89
Andromeda 90
Antares 118–19
Aquila 53, 89
Aristotle 48, 57, 73–4, 75, 77, 91, 100–1, 124, 135
astrology 123-9

Betelgeuse 42, 44, 88, 126, 127
Big Bang Theory 91–2
black holes 60
Blake, William 41, 92
Brahman 120
Bruno, Giordano 33, 76, 78
Buddha 19–20, 119
Buddhism 19, 40–1, 63, 140

Cancer 124, 128–9
Canopus 25
Caph 89, 90
carbon atoms 43, 45–6
Carina 25
Cassiopeia 89–90
Castor 126–7
chaos theory 94
comets 133, 134, 135–6
consciousness 119–21, 122
Copernicus, Nicolaus 28, 29–30, 37, 58, 73
creation 48, 63, 91, 92, 121, 140, 141
creative activity 49
curiosity 82–4
Cygnus 53, 61

darkness 84–6
Darwin, Erasmus 83
deep time 139–41
Deneb 53

eclipses 57, 70
Einstein, Albert 99–100, 102
Eratosthenes 57

feeling the earth turn 26–7, 37
future, the 93–5, 136, 138

Galileo 11–15, 25, 31, 48, 58, 73, 74, 115, 137
    comets 135–6
    gravity 73–4, 101
    horoscopes 123–4
    the Inquisition 12, 15, 23, 33, 75–9
    Milky Way 55, 56, 59
    moons of Jupiter 14, 31-3, 55
    speed of light 86–7
    tides 108–9
    writings 13, 34, 56, 78
Gemini 30–1, 32, 34–5, 36, 124, 126–8
God 40, 48, 62, 63, 70, 71, 84–5, 91, 92, 95, 120, 137
gravity 26, 42, 44, 45, 60, 73–4, 93, 97–109

Herschel, William 114
Hewish, Anthony 51
Hutchinson's Splendour of the Heavens 112–13

inertia 104-5

Jesus 21, 40, 47
Jupiter 31, 34–5, 36, 69, 72, 73
moons of 14, 31–3, 55, 116

Kepler, Johannes 74, 86, 104, 114, 124

Leo 124, 128–9
Leparia 66–71, 72, 78
letting go 77, 137
Levi, Primo 45
Lippershey, Hans 13–14, 31
Lowell, Percival 113–14
Lyra 42, 53, 56

Maria Celeste, Sister 13, 15, 79,
    123, 137
Mars 68–9, 72–5, 112–15, 116
meditation on a star 42–3
meteors 132–5
Milky Way 14, 52–6, 59–61, 63,
    90, 121
mindfulness 19–21
Moon, the 9–10, 14, 30, 74, 75, 88,
    114, 115, 128–9, 134
    Apollo missions 25, 101, 106–7
    eclipses 57, 70
    gardening by 108
    gravity 102–9
    Harvest Moon 102–3
    momentum 104–5
    tides 107–9
moral compass 122
mythology 33, 52, 53–4, 61, 114,
    120, 124, 126

Newton, Isaac 101–2, 104, 108

Orion 27, 42, 87–9, 126, 127

Perseids, the 133–4
Pleiades, the 126
Plough, the 67
Pluche, Noel Antoine: Nature
    Displayed 82, 84–5
Polaris 42, 67

Pope, Alexander 102
precession of the equinoxes 125
Psalm 104 25
Ptolemy 28, 58, 74

Regulus 128

Sagittarius 59–60
Saturn 73, 116
Schiaparelli, Giovanni 113
Scorpio 30, 118
Scott, Dave 101, 107
Segin 89–90
shooting stars 68, 132–3
Sirius 26, 88, 127
Southern Cross 24–5
speed of light 86–9, 121
star dust 44–5, 46, 61, 118
Sun, the 57–8, 59, 60, 61, 62, 73
    as centre of the solar system
        29–34, 72, 74, 75, 105, 109
    eclipses 70
    light from 88
    spots 14, 75

Taurus 31, 124, 125–6
telescope 13–14, 31, 55, 114
tides 107–9
Traherne, Thomas 41, 44

Vega 42, 53, 56, 61
Venus 14, 69, 115–16

Ward, Keith 120
Weil, Simone 95
Wells, H.G. 112
Wordsworth, William 55